Dancing Fish and Ammonites

Center Point
Large Print

Also by Penelope Lively and available from Center Point Large Print:

How It All Began

This Large Print Book carries the Seal of Approval of N.A.V.H.

Dancing Fish and Ammonites

A Memoir

PENELOPE LIVELY

CENTER POINT LARGE PRINT
THORNDIKE, MAINE

This Center Point Large Print edition is
published in the year 2014 by arrangement with
Viking, a member of Penguin Group (USA) LLC,
a Penguin Random House Company.

First published in Great Britain as
Ammonites and Leaping Fish by Fig Tree,
an imprint of Penguin Books Ltd.

Photographs by Anna Lively.

The text of this Large Print edition is unabridged.
In other aspects, this book may vary
from the original edition.
Printed in the United States of America
on permanent paper.
Set in 16-point Times New Roman type.

ISBN: 978-1-62899-054-6

Library of Congress Cataloging-in-Publication Data

Lively, Penelope, 1933–
 Dancing fish and ammonites : a memoir / Penelope Lively. — Center
point large print edition.
 pages ; cm
 ISBN 978-1-62899-054-6 (library binding : alk. paper)
 1. Lively, Penelope, 1933–
   2. Novelists, English—20th century—Biography.
   3. English literature—Women authors—Biography.
   4. Autobiographical memory. 5. Large type books. I. Title.
PR6062.I89Z46 2014b
823′.914—dc23
 [B]

2014000469

JACK—in memory

Contents

Preface

This is not quite a memoir. Rather, it is the view from old age.

And a view of old age itself, this place at which we arrive with a certain surprise—ambushed, or so it can seem. The view from eighty, for me. One of the few advantages of age is that you can report on it with a certain authority; you are a native now, and know what goes on here. That, and the backwards glance—the identifying freight of a lifetime.

A lifetime is embedded; it does not float free, it is tethered—to certain decades, to places, to people. It has a context; each departure leaves a person-shaped void—the absence within a family, the presence lost within a house, in a community, in society itself. We go, but hang in for a while in other people's heads—something we said, something we did; we leave a ghostly imprint on our backdrop. A very few people go one further and are distilled into a blue plaque on a building.

I began on a spring morning in the Anglo-American Hospital in Zamalek, which was a residential suburb on Gezira, the island in Cairo's Nile; 17 March 1933. Elsewhere, things were going on that would lead to turmoil in North

Africa in a few years' time; my parents' lives would be affected, and mine, but they were comfortably oblivious that morning, and I was tucked up in a crib, the feet of which stood in tin trays of water, because there had been instances of ants getting at newborn babies.

Toward the end of my own stint I find myself thinking less about what has happened to me but interested in this lifetime context, in the times of my life. I have the great sustaining ballast of memory; we all do, and hope to hang on to it. I am interested in the way that memory works, in what we do with it, and what it does with us. And when I look around my cluttered house—more ballast, material ballast—I can see myself oddly identified and defined by what is in it: my life charted out on the bookshelves, my concerns illuminated by a range of objects.

These, then, are the prompts for this book: age, memory, time, and this curious physical evidence I find all around me as to what I have been up to— how reading has fed into writing, how ways of thinking have been nailed.

There can be a certain detachment about it; the solipsism of writing about oneself tempered by the more compelling interest of general concerns—what it means to be old, what the long view does to us, or for us, how we mutate with our times. But a report from the front line has to be just that; this is my old age, so I have to get personal, as well as consider the wider implications of where I am now. Which is something I have not done before; like, I think, most people, I have not paid too much attention to old age. To individuals, yes—family, friends. But the status has not been on my radar. Give up my seat on the bus—of course; feign polite attention to some rambling anecdote; raise my voice, repeat myself with patience. Avoid, occasionally, I fear: that hazard light worn by the old—slow, potentially boring, hard going. Now that I wear the light myself, I am nicely aware of the status. This is a different place. And since I am there, along with plenty of my friends, the expedient thing seems to be to examine it. And report.

We are many today, in the Western world: the new demographic. I want to look at the implications of that, at the condition, at how it has been perceived. And then at the compelling matter of memory—the vapor trail without which we are undone.

And my own context—the context of anyone my age. The accompanying roar of the historical process. I want to remember what those events felt like at the time, those by which I felt most fingered—the Suez crisis, the Cold War, the seismic change in attitudes of the late twentieth century—and see how they are judged today, with the wisdoms of historical hindsight.

And, finally, some pure solipsism: one person's

life as reflected by possessions. Books; and a selection of things. Mine. But a story that anyone could tell; most of us end up with an identifying cargo—that painting, this vase, those titles on the shelf. I can give eloquence to mine—I know what they are saying. Not so much detachment here; more, a flicker of memoir proper—a voyage around the eighty years by way of two ammonites, a pair of American ducks, leaping fish . . . And a raft of books.

Old Age

Years ago, I heard Anthony Burgess speak at the Edinburgh Book Festival. He was impressive in that he spoke for an hour without a single note, fluent and coherent. But of the content of his talk all I remember are his opening words: "For me, death is already sounding its high C." This was around 1980, I think, so he was in his early sixties at the time, and died in 1993. I was in my late forties, and he seemed to me—not old, exactly, but getting on a bit.

Today, people in their sixties seem—not young, just nicely mature. Old age is in the eye of the beholder. I am eighty, so I am old, no question. The high C is audible, I suppose, but I don't pay it much attention. I don't think much about death. I am not exactly afraid of it, though after reading Julian Barnes's book *Nothing To Be Frightened Of*, with admiration, I felt that I had not sufficiently explored my own position on the matter but have perhaps arrived at the state of death-consciousness that he distinguishes with the argument that we cannot truly savor life without a regular awareness of extinction. Yes, I recognize that, along with the natural human taste for a conclusion: there has been a beginning, which proposes an end. I am afraid of the run-up to death, because I have had to watch that. But I think that many of us who are on the last lap are too busy with the baggage of old age to waste much time anticipating the finishing line. We have to get used to being the person we are, the person we have always been, but encumbered now with various indignities and disabilities, shoved as it were into some new incarnation. We feel much the same, but clearly are not. We have entered an unexpected dimension; dealing with this is the new challenge.

The extent of the challenge depends on when and where you experience old age. Social context is crucial. You don't want to be old when circumstances mean that anyone who doesn't contribute but requires support is a drag, and there is therefore a grim logic in failing to sustain them. Nomadic groups existing at subsistence level did better without the encumbrance of anyone who couldn't keep up. The district nurse in Ronald Blythe's *Akenfield* talks of the Suffolk cottages in the last century where a decaying grandparent was stacked away somewhere and nudged toward the grave. The anthropologist Colin Turnbull has given a horrific account in *The Mountain People* of the Ik, a Ugandan tribe whose flexible way of life was curtailed, forcing them to live in one area with insufficient resources, at starvation level. The effect was the erosion of any care or concern for others, with the old forced to starve first, and children also (further stark logic: keep the breeding group alive, you can always make more children if things improve). But the old, in this corner of Uganda in the mid-twentieth century, were around forty; "old" is never a fixed feast.

There is anthropological evidence from elsewhere that in a hunter-gatherer society the old are valued simply for experience—they have a bank of hunter-gatherer knowledge. That again makes sense; you may not be all that fond of Granny, but she knows where to find those roots you need. Elephant groups also depend on the matriarch, it seems, to know where to head for water and for food; I like this elemental link with animal behavior.

Things aren't quite like this in a world powered by technology; just as well that increased affluence means that nobody disposes of the aged just because they can't cope with a computer or a cell phone. Rather the contrary; at the time of writing there is a heated debate about the quality of care for the elderly in hospitals, and a scandal about conditions in a failing group of residential homes for old people. Things can go wrong, but it is beyond question that society assumes a responsibility toward the old; you don't leave them by the wayside, you don't push them into a cupboard and forget to feed them.

This may not be due entirely to a more

enlightened attitude. Old age is the new demographic, and you can't ignore the problems created by a group that has been getting steadily larger—alarmingly larger if you are in the business of allocating national expenditure. The poor have always been with us, and now the old are too.

We have not been, in the past, and we are not so much around still in some parts of the developing world. But in the West we are entrenched, bolstered by our pensions, brandishing our senior discount passes, cluttering up the doctors' offices, with an average life expectancy of around eighty. But our experience is one unknown to most of humanity, over time. We are the pioneers, as an established social group gobbling up benefits and giving grief to government agencies. Before the early modern period, as historians like to call it, before the sixteenth century, few people saw fifty, let alone eighty. Scroll back, and average life expectancy diminishes century by century; two thousand years ago, it stood at around twenty-five. That said, the old have always been around—it seems that perhaps eight percent of the population of medieval England was over sixty—but not as a significant demographic group, rather as noticeable individuals. And sixty today is not seen as old.

The Bible blithely allowed for threescore years and ten—where on earth did they get that from?

You'd be lucky indeed to make that in the Middle East in Roman times. Life expectancy is of course a slippery concept. The trick is to get through infancy, then the next four years; notch those up, and you're in with a fighting chance, your statistic rockets—if you are a medieval peasant (or in much of sub-Saharan Africa, or Afghanistan, today) you may well hang in there till forty or beyond. But chances are you won't leave toddler-hood; the underworld is a teeming sea of tiny ghosts, with, dotted among them, out of scale, inappropriate and incongruous, the exhausted figures of the old. Think Sparta (babies exposed on hillsides), think Coram's Fields (London hospital for foundlings), think Hogarth, think Dickens. Think *Kindertotenlieder*.

Archaeology recognizes old bones as likely to have been powerful bones. If you survived the demands of warrior culture and managed not to get picked off while leading the tribe into battle, then you got the lion's share of resources: food, creature comforts. Bones are intriguing, illuminating—this extraordinary surviving evidence of a life, for those who know how to read it. A recent television series did just that; an erudite expert homed in on a skeleton, and from it lifted the story of a Roman gladiator in first-century York, of the mother of triplets dying in childbirth, of the Iron Age sacrificial victim. Bones found in neolithic Orkney tombs indicate that people in their teens and twenties had osteoarthritis, brought on presumably by some repetitive physical activity (hauling all that stone around for the tombs, maybe). And I wince—arthritic young are an affront. But I am making the mistake of assuming a twenty-first-century perspective; these were not young, in their terms, or, rather, a lifespan was not long enough for the luxury of the seven ages of man—just an instant of childhood, a brief flare of maturity, and then into the chambered tomb with the ancestors.

A recent survey by the UK's Department of Work and Pensions, which is somewhat obsessed with the question of old age, for good reason, found that most believe that old age starts at fifty-nine while youth ends at forty-one. People over eighty, on the other hand, believe sixty-eight to herald old age, while fifty-two is the end of youth. Of course, of course—it depends where you happen to be standing yourself. And youth has expanded handsomely since Charlotte Brontë wailed, "I am now thirty-two. Youth is gone—gone,—and will never come back; can't help it." It still won't come back, even after a century and a half of scientific advance, but there is plenty of remedial work on offer by way of nipping and tucking for those feeling a bit desperate. The rest of us settle for the inevitable sag and wrinkle, and simply adjust our concept of the climactic points. Actually, I'd step out of line and go for seventy rather than sixty-eight as the brink of old age; I have too many vigorous and active friends in their late sixties and anyway the round number is neater.

By 2030 there will be four million people over eighty in the United Kingdom—out of a population of around sixty million. No wonder the Department of Work and Pensions is getting rattled on behalf of its successors. I will have handed in my dinner pail and my transit pass by then, I sincerely hope, though I can't quite count on it. I come from a horribly long-lived family. My mother died at ninety-three; her brother made it to one hundred; their mother reached ninety-seven. I look grimly at these figures; I do not wish to compete.

Suffice it that we are too many. That's one way of looking at it: the administrative point of view, the view perhaps sometimes of the young, who have inherited the world, quite properly, and may occasionally find themselves guilty of the ageist sentiments that are now proscribed. Actually, I haven't much come up against ageism, myself. There was an occasion, I remember, a few years ago, when a teenage granddaughter was advising on the acquisition of a cell phone and the salesman's enthusiastic attention turned to disdain when he realized that the purchase was not for her but for the old granny, who had no business with any mobile device, let alone the latest Nokia. But more usually I find that age has bestowed a kind of comfortable anonymity. We are not especially interesting, by and large—waiting for a bus, walking along the street; younger people are busy sizing up one another, in the way that children in a park will only register other children. We are not exactly invisible, but we are not noticed, which I rather like; it leaves me free to do what a novelist does anyway, listen and watch, but with the added spice of feeling a little as though I am some observant time-traveler, on the edge of things, bearing witness to the customs of another age. I am dramatizing, of course—I am still a part of it all and most of what I see and hear is entirely familiar because as society mutates—language, behavior—so have I mutated, in assumptions and expectations. This is something I want to talk about in a later section—the way in which you change your skin, over a lifetime, change and change again. The point here is that age may sideline, but it also confers a sort of neutrality; you are no longer out there in the thick of things, but able to stand back, observe, consider.

The other view, the counterview to the administrators and the ageists, is that this is the human race adapting again, and how interesting. How significant, how challenging that there is now this new demographic, this hefty group of people who have notched up seven or eight decades and counting, many of whom are still in good health, with all their marbles, able to savor life.

Up to a point, that is. I am a diarist. It is a working diary, mainly, in which I jot down stuff that might possibly come in useful at some point. This means that I can never find anything I think I may once have noted, but during a trawl recently I came upon my visit to a specialist in 1994, around the time the spinal arthritis first struck that has plagued me ever since. " 'Anno Domini, I'm afraid,' says the man kindly. 'Whoever designed us didn't make sufficient allowance for wear and tear.' Which chimed nicely with my view of the Great Designer in the Sky—a piece of malevolent sabotage to ensure that when the human race gets to the point of discovering penicillin and sanitation and generally prolonging life those prolonged won't find it worth living anyway."

I beg to differ, eighteen years on. One does; today, and for a while, perhaps. Most of my friends of my age group would agree, I think, and most of them have been slammed with something: hips, knees, teeth, eyes . . . We do indeed wear out before our time. The science of aging is complex and intriguing. The gerontologist Tom Kirkwood gives a technical but lively account in his book *Time of Our Lives*. He quotes John Maynard Smith's dry definition: "Ageing is a progressive, generalized impairment of function resulting in an increasing probability of death." Quite. But what is going on? Why do we age?

The short answer seems to be: because we are disposable. And we are disposable because our own genes have decided this; their interests in keeping us going do not coincide with our own. The maintenance of certain cells most affected by the aging process takes many resources. If this is reduced, then energy is released for growth and reproduction, so natural selection favors such a mutation. This is called the "disposable soma" theory; my digest of it is inadequate—please go to Professor Kirkwood for a proper account. There is a cool rationality to the process (of course, natural selection is always rational) and while this is not exactly a palliative (it remains a natural response to "Rage, rage against the dying of the light") at least you can see what it's all about. And what would be the alternative? Swift's Struldbrugs in *Gulliver's Travels*, born to immortality, were condemned to an eternity of senile decay and estrangement from society. They presumably suffered from some genetic derangement; I think we must prefer genetic normality and accept the consequences.

Society is stuck with us, I'm afraid, and it will get worse. In countries with high life expectancies, a third of today's children may reach one hundred. In 1961 there were just five hundred and ninety-two people over the age of one hundred in this country; by 2060 there will be four hundred and fifty-five thousand. Consider those figures, and gasp. Old people were of interest in the past simply because there weren't that many of them—the sage is a pejorative term suggesting that old age necessarily implies wisdom. That view may have changed radically toward the end of the twenty-first century, I'd guess, when the Western world is awash with centenarians. Goodness knows what that will do for attitudes toward the elderly; I'm glad I shan't be around to find out. I am concerned with here and now, when I can take stock and bear witness.

One of the few advantages of writing fiction in old age is that you have been there, done it all, experienced every decade. I can remember worrying when I was writing at forty, at fifty, that I didn't know what it was like to be seventy, eighty, if I wanted to include an older character. Well, I didn't know what it was like to be a man, either, but you have to stick your neck out—use empathy, imagination, observation, all the novelist's tools. But it is certainly a help to have acquired that long backwards view; not only do you know (even if it is getting a bit hazy) what it felt like to be in your twenties, or thirties, but you remember also the relative unconcern about what was to come.

You aren't going to get old, of course, when you are young. We won't ever be old, partly because we can't imagine what it is like to be old, but also because we don't want to, and—crucially—are not particularly interested. When I was a teenager, I spent much time with my Somerset grandmother, then around seventy. She was a brisk and applied grandmother who was acting effectively as a mother-substitute; I was devoted to her, but I don't remember ever considering what it could be like to *be* her. She simply *was;* unchangeable, unchanging, in her tweed skirt, her blouse, her Shetland cardigan, her suit for Sunday church, worn with chenille turban, her felt hat for shopping trips. Her opinions that had been honed in the early part of the century; her horror of colors that "clashed;" her love of Tchaikovsky, Beethoven, Berlioz. I never thought about how it must be to be her; equally, I couldn't imagine her other than she was, as though she had sprung thus into life, had never been young.

Old age is forever stereotyped. Years ago, I was a judge for a national children's writing competition. They had been asked to write about "grandparents"; in every offering the grandparent was a figure with stick and hearing aid, knitting by the fireside or pottering in the garden. The average grandparent would then have been around sixty, and probably still at work. When booking a rail ticket by phone recently, I found myself shifted from the automated voice to a real person when I had said I had a Senior Railcard, presumably on the grounds that I might get muddled and require help—which was kind, I suppose, but I was managing quite well. We are too keen to bundle everyone by category; as a child, I used to be maddened by the assumption that I would get along famously with someone just because we were both eight.

All that we have in common, we in this new demographic, are our aches and pains and disabilities—and, yes, that high C evoked by Anthony Burgess. For the rest of it, we are the people we have always been—splendidly various, and let us respect that. The young are in control, which is as it should be, and mostly we wouldn't wish to be out there now taking the flak, though there have always been majestic exceptions, with politicians the high fliers: think Churchill, prime minister at eighty, think Gladstone, think Bismarck. But we do not wish to be arbitrarily retired, or to have assumptions made about our capacities and our tastes, and since we are likely in years to come to make significant demands on national resources, then it would make sense to make use of us for as long as we are fit, able and willing to contribute. How you set about this I wouldn't care to say—I am a novelist, not a think tank; some sharp young minds could surely apply themselves to the matter.

"Go West, young man, go West." The second part of that exhortation usually gets left out: ". . . and grow up with the country." I sometimes think of that when noting the influx of young foreign males in my part of London—the Polish builders busy making over my neighbors' houses; the teams of two, shoving fliers through the doors, chatting away in some language I can't identify; those loud on their cell phones as they pass me in the street (is that Bulgarian? Czech? Russian?). I have had many an interesting conversation with minicab drivers, apparently arrived in this country a month ago and already whisking around the city: "Where are you living?" "I am in Lewisham. There is house that is all Afghan mans. Pity is no Afghan womans." "What do you think of London?" "Is pity is so many old building, but they put up new I see, perhaps in time the old go." "How did you get here . . ." No, best not to pursue the matter.

These resourceful young are not going to grow up with a new country, but are cashing in on an old one, and you cannot but admire them. That takes courage, determination—and sometimes desperation. And, of course, youth. You don't plunge into an alien city, you don't stow away in a cargo truck, unless you have that panache, that as yet unstifled optimism, that ingrained sense that the road ahead is there, still there.

"The party's nearly over," says a friend and contemporary; she says it a touch ruefully, but gamely also. We have had a party; we've been luckier than many. And we are attuned to the idea of life as a narrative—everyone is. Just as the young Afghan knows his story has only just begun—and he is hell-bent on seeing that it continues—so we take a kind of wry satisfaction in recognizing the fit and proper progress, the shape of things. The sense of an ending.

The trajectory of life, the concept of universal death, conditions our thinking. We require things to end, to mirror our own situation. The idea of infinity is impossible to grasp. When I am invited to do so, watching one of those television programs about the expanding universe, with much fancy computerized galaxy performance on the screen, and sober explications from Californian astrophysicists, I can't, frankly. And what is intriguing is that they too, while evidently accepting the concept in a stern professional physicist way, seem also to have an ordinary human resistance. Last time, two of them said "mind-boggling," reaching helplessly, it seemed, for that most jaded cliché to account for something that is beyond language. They couldn't find words for it; neither can I.

I have had much to do with endings, as a writer of fiction. The novel moves from start to finish, as does the short story; at the outset, the conclusion lurks—where is this thing going? how will I wrap it up? how will I give it a satisfactory shape? You are looking to supply the deficiencies of reality, to provide order where life is a matter of contingent chaos, to suggest theme and meaning, to make a story that is shapely where life is linear. "Tick-tock": Frank Kermode's famous "model of what we call a plot, an organization that humanizes time by giving it form." The need to give significance to simple chronicity: "All such plotting presupposes and requires that an end will bestow upon the whole duration and meaning." This is the satisfaction of a successful work of fiction—the internal coherence that reality does not have. Life as lived is disordered, undirected and at the mercy of contingent events. I wrote a novel recently which mirrored this process but tried also to make a point about the effects of the process, which seemed like having it both ways and was fiendishly difficult to do, and that served me right, but it was a chance to explore the alarming interdependence that directs our lives.

We have this need for narrative, it seems. A life is indeed a "tick-tock": birth and death with nothing but time in between. We go to fiction because we like a story, and we want our lives to have the largesse of story, the capacity, the onward thrust—we not only want, but need, which is why memory is so crucial, and without it we are lost, adrift in a hideous eternal present. The compelling subject of memory is for another section of this book; the point here is simply that we cannot but see the trajectory from youth to old age as a kind of story—my story, your story—and the backwards gaze of old age is much affected by the habits of fiction. We look for the sequential comforts of narrative—this happened, then that; we don't care for the arbitrary. My story—your story—is a matter of choice battling with contingency: "The best-laid schemes o' mice an' men . . ." We are well aware of that, but the retrospective view would still like a bit of fictional elegance. For some, psychoanalysis perhaps provides this—explanations, understandings. Most of us settle for the disconcerting muddle of what we intended and what came along, and try to see it as some kind of whole.

That said, it remains difficult to break free of the models supplied by fiction. "The preference for progress is a basic assumption of the *Bildungsroman* and the upward mobility story, and an important component of much comedy, romance, fairy tale," writes Helen Small in her magisterial investigation of old age as viewed in philosophy and literature, *The Long Life*. "It is also an element in the logic of tragedy: one of the reasons tragedy (certain kinds, at least) is painful is that it affronts the human desire for progress." We are conditioned by reading, by film, by drama, with, it occurs to me, long-running television soaps being the only salutary reminder of what real life actually does—it goes on and on as a succession of events until the plug is pulled;

we should note the significance of *Coronation Street* and *EastEnders*. We want some kind of identifiable progress, a structure, and the only one is the passage of time, the notching up of decades until the exit line is signaled.

Helen Small has written also of the debate—usually between philosophers, it seems—about the concept of eternal life. Is death in fact desirable? A moot point indeed, and of course it depends on what sort of life you suppose—some kind of imagined eternal youth or the inevitable decline we all know and do not love but recognize. Swift's Struldbrugs seem to me to have had the last word. And the very euphemism we use for death—an end—seems to reflect our fictional conditioning, our sense of an ending. It is appropriate, that end.

Appropriate in theory, though we view it without enthusiasm. The thing that most vexes me about the prospect of my end is that I shan't know what comes after, not just—in fact, perhaps least of all—in the grand scale of things but on my own immediate horizon: how will life unroll for my grandchildren? What will they make of it? I shall be written out of the story (like disposable actors in soap operas), and my story is hitched to many other stories. Every life is tangled with a multitude of other lives, again in a perverse mix of choice and contingency. You choose partners and friends; you don't choose those you end up working with, or living next door to. Either way, your story has wound in with theirs, and because of this you can be wrong-footed by your own existence. There is existence as it has seemed to you, and there are those other versions served up by other people. You think it was like this; your parent, child, discarded lover, professional rival, says no, the view from here is subtly different.

I shall never know the view from my grand-children, which may be just as well. And the discordant aspects of any life are of course the stuff of fiction—the ambiguities, the contra-dictions. When it comes to reality, plenty are anxious to get in a preemptive strike by way of autobiography and memoir, especially those who have been on the public stage and are well aware that they are going to get a good going-over in due course; there can't be many politicians who have not spent their declining years honing their version of things before it is too late.

There is a vogue for "life writing" at the moment, both for publication and as private endeavors. I am all for it, partly because I gobble up other people's lives, as a reader, but also because it seems to me a productive personal exercise—to stand aside and have a look at your story and try, not to make sense of it, which may be too taxing, but to trace the narrative thread, to look at the roads not taken, to see where you began and where you have got to. An exercise also in solipsism, perhaps, but we are all solipsistic, and actually the exercise itself demands as well a measure of detachment.

There is one thing missing, of course, from personal life writing: that requisite ending. Tick without the tock. I would find that most unsettling, were I to attempt any sort of conventional memoir (which I shan't do); the novelist in me requires that tension between start and finish, the sense of a whole, of a progress towards conclusion. But I am quite at home with the idea of my life—any life—as a bit-player in the lives of others; that is the stuff of fiction, again, and the challenge of any novel is to find a balance for the relationships within the cast list, to make these interesting, intriguing, to have them shift and perhaps unravel over the course of the narrative. So that side of things is fine; fact and fiction nicely reflect one another. It is the search for an ending that is the problem.

Which takes me back to the prompt for this digression: the parabola between youth and age, and the way in which it conditions the view in winter. The winter of old age is not going to give way to spring, so the term is inept, but it suits the static nature of old age, the sense that things have wound down, gone into suspension. The party's nearly over, yes, and that euphemistic ending is somewhere just over the horizon, but in the meantime there is this new dimension of life—often demanding, sometimes dismaying, always worth examining.

Am I envious of the young? Would I want to be young again? On the first count—not really, which surprises me. On the second—certainly not, if it meant a repeat performance. I would like to have back vigor and robust health, but that is not exactly envy. And, having known youth, I'm well aware that it has its own traumas, that it is no Elysian progress, that it can be a time of distress and disappointment, that it is exuberant and exciting, but it is no picnic. I don't particularly want to go back there.

And in any case, I am someone else now. This seems to contradict earlier assertions that you are in old age the person you always were. What I mean is that old age has different needs, different satisfactions, a different outlook. I remember my young self, and I am not essentially changed, but I perform otherwise today.

There are things I no longer want, things I no longer do, things that are now important. I have no further desire whatsoever for travel. What? No further desire? You who crossed the Atlantic twice a year or so? Who left Heathrow twelve times one year? Who was happy to hop off pretty much anywhere at the behest of the British Council or on book-related business? Who went on holidays?

That's right; absolutely no further desire, and that includes holidays. I never want to see another airport. And, furthermore, I don't miss it. Maybe I wouldn't feel like this if I had not done so much—been there, seen that—if I didn't have it stashed away in my head, though the random retrieval system means that only some of it floats up. A sudden glimpse of those ring-tailed lemurs in Melbourne Zoo, and the publisher's office in Ljubljana where I was given the Slovenian translation of "Jabberwocky"; the audience member at a reading in New York Public Library who had brought me a red rose from her garden. The summers with friends in Maine and Massachusetts. I have it—at least, I have shreds of it—and that will do nicely.

All right, this is the diminishment of old age. I don't want to travel anymore because I know I couldn't do it now, and perhaps there is some benign mechanism that aligns diminished capacity with diminished desire. Though I'm not sure—contemporaries have disputed this: they do miss travel, they resent being grounded. And some of them are not—still braving Terminal Four, still sitting squashed in a metal canister with hundreds of others for hours on end, still, I suppose, getting that adrenaline rush. Perhaps I have just given in to diminishment, or, I prefer to think, I have simply made a choice. I don't want to do it anymore.

Domestic travel is another matter. I still get around the UK, but I don't regard that as travel—that is simply checking out the territory, discovering, revisiting, crossing my own path, and I wouldn't be without it. A number of years ago the railway authorities, with a sudden rush of indulgence, decided that senior citizens should be allowed tickets to anywhere at non-peak times for five pounds, I think it was. I remember finding myself on an east coast train surrounded by jubilant gray heads, busy racking up all the mileage they could. That offer was withdrawn, in a panic, after a month or so. That'll teach them.

So, domestic travel only for me now. I am nicely smug, where my carbon footprint is concerned. What else do I not want to do anymore? Go to anything about which I am unenthusiastic. Time was, I attended hither and thither, frequently out of compunction: I really ought to show up. Or I thought: come on, give it a go, you never know . . . Not now. It is pure self-interest, today. I attend only when I think I will probably enjoy this. Out with all those speculative sorties to some event or gathering; far more alluring is the evening with a couple of hours reading and maybe some TV if there's anything with promise. I can—just barely—remember how it was to be twenty with the horror of a blank evening ahead, nothing to go to, no company lined up. I can remember what that felt like, I can remember myself feeling, but this is the sense in which I am someone else now.

This someone else, this alter ego who has arrived, is less adventurous, more risk-averse, protective of her time. Well, of course—there is the matter of the spirit and the flesh, and that is the crux of it: the spirit is still game for experience, anything on offer, but the body most definitely is not, and unfortunately calls the shots. My mind seems to be holding out—so far, so good. My poor father had Alzheimer's; that shadow lies over all of my age group, with the numbers of sufferers now rising all the time—but that is of course a factor of the new demographic. Dementia is irreversible and you can't fend it off, though it seems that exercise and a healthy balanced diet can help to do so, along with regular brain activity such as crosswords and sudoku. I am not a crossword addict and sudoku defeats me entirely; I must put my trust in writing novels and, maybe, this.

Writing is not a problem, thankfully. The language arrives, the word I want. I have never much used a thesaurus, and don't do so now. But here's an odd thing—words remain biddable, but names do not. Names drop into a black hole—the leader of the opposition, that actor I saw last week, the acquaintance who comes up at a party. After a while Ed Miliband will surface, and I dance around the problem of the acquaintance by avoiding introductions. I'm not worried, because I know I'm not alone—my contemporaries all have the same complaint. But why names and not words? Nothing that I have yet read on the operation of memory or the function of the brain in old age has yet offered an explanation; answers in comprehensible detail, please. A friend says: it's because we've known, and known of, so many people—we have name overload by now. I am aware that there is a condition that makes sufferers unable to remember the word they are after—aphasia; Kingsley Amis had some wry fun with it in his novel *Ending Up*. But the name difficulty seems to be generic, and I'm skeptical about my friend's explanation.

Writing survives, for me. Other pleasures—needs—do not. I was a gardener. Well, I am a gardener, but a sadly reduced one, in every sense. I have a small paved rectangle of London garden, full of pots, with a cherished twenty-year-old corokia, and two pittosporums, and various fuchsias, and *Convolvulus cneorum* and hakonechloa grass and euphorbia and heuchera and a *Hydrangea petiolaris* all over the back wall (well, some of you will be gardeners and might share my tastes). It gives me much pleasure, but is a far cry from what I once gardened—a half acre or so that included a serious vegetable garden: potatoes, onions, all the beans, carrots, squash, you name it, the lot. All I can do now is potter with the hose in summer, and do a bit of snipping here and there, thanks to the arthritis; forget travel, what I really do miss is intensive gardening. Digging, raking, hoeing—the satisfactory creation of a trench for the potatoes, deft work with the hoe around a line of young French beans, the texture of rich, well-fertilized soil. Pruning a shaggy rose: shaping for future splendor. Dividing fat clumps of snowdrops: out of many shall come more still. And that was—is—the miraculous power of gardening: it evokes tomorrow, it is eternally forward-looking, it invites plans and ambitions, creativity, expectation. Next year I will try celeriac. And that new pale blue sweet pea. Would *Iris stylosa* do just here? And what about sweet woodruff in that shady corner? Gardening defies time; you labor today in the interests of tomorrow; you think in seasons to come, cutting down the border this autumn but with next spring in your mind's eye. And I still have something of this, in my London patch; twice a year, my daughter takes me to a garden center for the seasonal splurge—the summer geraniums, the pansies for winter.

An addiction to gardening is genetic, I believe. My grandmother gardened to the exclusion of almost everything else; my mother had the gene, and now my daughter has it too. A working musician, she acquired Royal Horticultural Society qualifications in spare time that she did not really have. I wish I had done that—I admire and envy her more informed way of gardening.

All the discussion of how to confront old age focuses on physical and mental activity. We must not subside into the armchair and pack up; we should go for a brisk walk every day (hips and knees permitting), we should reach for the crossword, pick up a book. There is much said about attitude, too. Those who had a positive attitude toward old age when in their fifties and sixties have been found to display a more sprightly outlook when it arrives. Well, I dare say, and that is really just a matter of diversity; some of us are like that, others are not. You are exhorted to be positive when you have cancer, with the underlying suggestion that if you don't your chances will be that much worse. Hmmm. A positive view may well do much for the state of mind, but I doubt if it affects the disease.

Something of the same applies to old age—condition not disease. A positive attitude is not going to cure the arthritis or the macular degeneration or whatever but a bit of bravado makes endurance more possible. Not everyone can manage this—diversity again. And bravado comes a great deal easier to those cushioned by financial security; I am intensely aware of this. There's something else, though, and that is not so much state of mind as what the mind in question is up to, indeed, whether it is up to anything at all. Friends in my age group who are successfully facing down old age are busy; several are hampered by hips, knees, etc. but still pursue their interests and activities. I know I have a fairly left-field range of friends, nearly all of whom have earned their bread through brain work, and nobody forces a writer into retirement (except incompliant publishers), but there does seem to be some staying power bestowed by . . . what? Curiosity? Mental energy? Perseverance? A surviving drive to seize the day? Any, I think—and all.

Can't garden. Don't want to travel. But can read, must read. For me, reading is the essential palliative, the daily fix. Old reading, revisiting, but new reading too, lots of it, reading in all directions, plenty of fiction, history, and archaeology always, reading to satisfy perennial tastes, reading sideways too—try her, try him, try that, Amazon and AbeBooks would founder without me; my house is a book depository—books in, books out (to family and friends, to my daughter's Somerset cottage where there is still some shelf space, to wonderful Book Aid which sends English-language books to places where they are needed). I buy; I am sent. Publishers send what my husband used to call "bread upon the waters" books to people like me: "We'd love to know if you enjoy this book as much as we have . . ." I can't read each one, but I always have a good look. Any book represents effort, struggle, work—

I know, I write them myself—every book deserves attention, even if that ends with dismissal. And occasionally there is gold: today the postman hands over Robert Macfarlane's latest, *The Old Ways*. Ah, discerning editor! I have devoured and reread Macfarlane's earlier books.

Reading in old age is doing for me what it has always done—it frees me from the closet of my own mind. Reading fiction, I see through the prism of another person's understanding; reading everything else, I am traveling—I am traveling in the way that I still can: new sights, new experiences. I am reminded sometimes of the intensity of childhood reading, that absolute absorption when the very ability to read was a heady new gain, the gateway to a different place, to a parallel universe you hadn't known was there. The one entirely benign mind-altering drug. Except of course for those who ban or burn books, in which case benign doesn't come into it, but the power of books is all the more acknowledged.

So I have my drug, perfectly legal and I don't need a prescription. Over the last few years, I have considered nature and nurture with Matt Ridley, explored Hengeworld with Mike Pitts, enjoyed centuries of British landscape with Francis Pryor, discovered France with Graham Robb. Plus a raft of novels and an expedient injection of poetry. More later on a lifetime of reading and the way in which reading has powered writing. My point here is to do with the needs of old age; there is what you can't do, there is what you no longer want to do, and there is what has become of central importance. Others may have a game of bowls, or baking cakes, or carpentry, or macramé, or watercolors. I have reading.

Writing this chapter, I have sometimes felt that I am eerily attuned to the thought processes of 10 Downing Street, where clearly some are much exercised about the new demographic. This morning the paper tells me that one of Prime Minister David Cameron's advisers says that elderly people should be encouraged to go back to work and move into smaller houses. It is not their welfare alone with which he is concerned; he wants their family-sized houses for the next generation, while to advance the retirement age would of course have an impact on the ever-increasing pension bill, though he masks this by insisting that the elderly need the social contact supplied by work—many of the old complain of isolation. True enough, I'm sure, and apparently the Swedish prime minister has floated the idea of seventy-five as a potential retirement age. The prospect of a future in which a great swathe of a nation's resources has to be set aside for the sustenance of an entirely inactive slab of the population is indeed challenging. But seventy-five-year-old refuse collectors? Seventy-five-year-olds digging the roads, erecting scaffolds? I don't think so. Office work, maybe, and indeed all those occupations without an element of physical labor. Many septuagenarians might well welcome that. I hope the Swedish prime minister has thought this through, and indeed our own, who has apparently said that he loves the idea of an automatic "life expectancy based adjustment" to the state pension age—which is already due to go up from sixty-five to sixty-eight over the next three decades. This is all very well, and I've advocated finding a means for those elderly who are able and keen to be useful to continue to be so, but the increased expectancy will have to be accompanied by increasingly robust hips, knees and everything else.

Professor Tom Kirkwood has written: "There is a little progress with age-related diseases." But he went on to say that in his study of a group over eighty-five not one had zero age-related disease, and most had four or five. Doctors' offices and hospital waiting rooms are well stocked with those over sixty-five; it is the old and the young who demand most attention. On a trip to University College Hospital Accident and Emergency a couple of years ago my companions in the waiting room were seven elderly men and women, and three mothers with babies or toddlers, all of us supervised by a stern-faced security man in case we started causing trouble. My visit was purely precautionary, insisted on by my doctor: I appreciated the resources and the efficiency but felt very much that I was indeed cluttering up the system.

Well, we do, and we can't help it. Over the last years, I have had surgery and treatment for breast cancer; hips and knees are holding out so far but my back gave in long ago: I have been in intermittent pain for fifteen years—discomfort always, tipping into real pain. My sight is dodgy—myopic macular degeneration, which may get worse (but also—fingers crossed—may not). There is a shoulder problem—a torn tendon. The worst was a cracked vertebra, four years ago, which required surgery—balloon kyphoplasty—which left me in intense, unrelenting, and apparently inexplicable pain for three and a half months. Pain that had the specialists shaking their heads, baffled, passing me around like the unwelcome parcel in that children's game—and I am sorry, apologetic, through the miasma of pain, sorry to be such a challenge, but sorrier still for myself. I want my life back. I want to be able to sit, stand, walk to the supermarket, watch the TV, meet a friend. Write my novel. We have run through the entire repertoire of pain-killers, starting with kindly and ineffective paracetamol and ibuprofen, moving through flirtations with co-codamol, Voltarol, the fentanyl patch . . . We are on to the hard stuff now; morphine turns me into a madwoman, so we don't go there again, but Demerol gives temporary relief. Demerol is—or was—used in childbirth; I remember it under different circumstances. But it works for about an hour and a half, and you can only take it every four hours. So, the blissful float into a hazy pain-distanced zone, and then back to reality, and watching the clock. Over those dreadful months, I wanted to see, talk to, only my children, and two friends. And my physical therapist—superb professional, practical, breezy, funny, convinced that we'll beat this: "You *will* get better."

I did. At last.

I have sometimes wondered if an experience like that has some salutary value for any of us: it puts into perspective subsequent distresses. As for the rest of my continuing ailments, they seem more or less par for the course for an eighty-year-old; of those I know in my age group, most can chalk up a few, or more, with only one or two that I can think of maddeningly unscathed.

You get used to it. And that surprises me. You get used to diminishment, to a body that is stalled, an impediment? Well, yes, you do. An alter ego is amazed, aghast perhaps—myself in the roaring forties, when robust health was an assumption, a given, something you barely noticed because it was always there. Acceptance has set in, somehow, has crept up on you, which is just as well, because the alternative—perpetual rage and resentment—would not help matters. You are now this other person, your earlier selves are out there, familiar, well remembered, but you have to come to terms with a different incarnation.

"In seventy or eighty years a Man may have a deep Gust of the World. Know what it is, what it can afford, and what 'tis to have been a Man." Reading Sir Thomas Browne, today, on a winter London afternoon, I'm in touch with a former self, who was discovering *Urne-Buriall* in Jack's set of the Works, in Oxfordshire in the 1970s: "The treasures of time lie high, in Urnes, Coynes and Monuments, scarce below the roots of some vegetables." Today, I am warming to Browne's discussion of the long view: ". . . such a compass of years will shew new examples of old things, parallelisms of occurrences through the whole course of Time, and nothing be monstrous unto him, who may in that time understand not only the varieties of Man, but the varieties of himself, and how many Men he hath been in that extent of time." Yes, yes—exactly. And how strange, how exciting, to find an echo of what I have been thinking about myself in that wonderful seventeenth-century mind. Back in my forties, I was responding to Browne's archaeological interests, being that way inclined myself, and relishing, always, always, that language—the cadences, the flourished word, the music.

". . . the varieties of himself"; perfect phrase.

And it is of the varieties of myself that I am aware, seeing how today's response to Browne links me to that Oxfordshire self, in mid-life, busy with children, but essentially the same person. The body may decline, may seem a dismal reflection of what went before, but the mind has a healthy continuity, and some kind of inbuilt fidelity to itself, a coherence over time. We learn, and experience; attitudes and opinions may change, but most people, it seems to me, retain an essential persona, a cast of mind, a trademark footprint. It is not so much that we simply get more like ourselves, as has been said, but that the self in question may expand, mutate, over time, but retains always that signature identity. A poet's voice will alter and develop, but young Wordsworth, Tennyson, Larkin are not essentially adrift from their later selves. There is this interesting accretion—the varieties of ourselves—and the puzzling thing in old age is to find yourself out there as the culmination of all these, knowing that they are you, but that you are also now this someone else.

Simone de Beauvoir confronted the problem in her extensive study *Old Age*: "Old age is particularly difficult to assume because we have always regarded it as something alien, a foreign species: 'Can I have become a different being while I still remain myself?'" What is at issue, it seems to me, is a new and disturbing relationship with time. It is as though you advanced along a plank hanging over a canyon: once, there was a long reassuring stretch of plank ahead; now there is plank behind, plenty of it, but only a few plank paces ahead. Once, time was the distance into which you peered—misty, impenetrable, with no discernible landmarks, but reassuringly *there*. In old age, that dependable distance has been whisked suddenly behind you—and it does seem to have happened suddenly. Not long ago, there was some kind of balance—a fore and aft, as it were. No longer; time has looped back, regressed, it no longer lies ahead, but behind. It has turned into something else, something called memory, and we need it—oh dear me, yes, we need it—but it is dismaying to have lost that sense of expectation, of anticipation. Not only that, but we are aware of the change in ourselves—we are the same, but different, and equipped now with a comet trail of completed time, the memory trail.

The mind does not always keep up—the subconscious, rather. In dreams, I am not always the self of today; I am often young, or younger, and if my children are present they have often become children again, obligingly—we have all jumped backwards. The mind cannot bear too much reality, it seems; in the same way, Jack is nearly always present in my dreams—it is twelve years since he died, but at night he returns, not always recognizably himself, but a shadowy dream companion figure that I always know to be him.

When Simone de Beauvoir published *Old Age* in 1970 she was sixty-two, so from my viewpoint she was barely even on the approach road to the status itself. And, indeed, her own life experience is hardly cited at all in her long, densely researched, somewhat impassioned and rather wonderful book, which remains an illuminating investigation of the subject. She embarked on this, she says, because she saw a conspiracy of silence about old age, as though all were in denial, refusing to anticipate their own future, and, in consequence, choosing to ignore the situation of the old. She cited the appalling poverty and state neglect of the old in France and in the United States. But the book goes far beyond indignation. She wanted to explore the way in which old age is not just a biological but a cultural fact, and to that end she delved into ethnology. She plowed through history to see how the old had got on, from classical Greece to the present day, she pursued evidence of attitudes toward old age. She searched out the voices of the old. The book is laced with references from art and literature, from sociology, psychology, philosophy. It is compendious, exhaustive, extremely serious— there's no light touch, with de Beauvoir—and impressive. She died at seventy-eight, so she got there herself—in 1986 you would certainly be considered old at seventy-eight.

Whether or not she turned the analytic eye on her own old age, she eventually had a grim experience of it, managing the care of Jean-Paul Sartre in his wretched decline into infirmity and blindness. A harsh diminishment, for these two intellectual heavyweights, and nicely reflecting all that she had written of the alienation from oneself that is the condition of old age.

I am sharing old age with friends, but not with a partner. In that, my situation is entirely average: three in five women over seventy-five in this country live alone. The men go first. Jack knew that, and expected it; after his retirement, he spent much time organizing our affairs, and would talk routinely of a future that excluded him, to my irritation. I would remonstrate, and he would smile amiably: "Statistics . . ." Well, he was right—though cheated, statistically, since he died at sixty-nine. The world is full of widows—several among my closer friends. We have each known that grim rite of passage, have engaged with grief and loss, and have not exactly emerged but found a way of living after and beyond. It is an entirely changed life, for anyone who has been in a long marriage—forty-one years, for me: alone in bed, alone most of the time, without that presence towards which you turned for advice, reassurance, with whom you shared the good news and the bad. Every decision now taken alone; no one to defuse anxieties. And a thoroughly commonplace experience—everywhere, always—so get on with it and don't behave as though you are uniquely afflicted. I didn't tell myself that at the time, and I doubt if it would have helped if I had, but it is what I have come—not so much to feel as to understand.

A common experience—like old age itself, for those fortunate enough (if that is the right word) to get there. Here we are—the eighty-somethings—around 1.4 million of us in the UK, most of us with nothing much in common except the accretion of years, a historical context, and a generous range of ailments from which we have probably been allocated two or three. For each of us the experience is different, each of us endures—or challenges—it differently. Both endurance and challenge will of course be more successful from the vantage point of financial security, and if you are not too encumbered on the ailment front. My own mood can vary from day to day—glum if it is a bad back day, buoyant the next if that is better, there's something interesting to look forward to, and the new tulips are out in the garden. But none of us escapes the daily challenge of the condition—so often newly surprising. However did I get like this? What happened?

Age and infirmity; portmanteau phrase, like law

and order. But apt, unfortunately. We are indeed infirm, and the main reason for that is loss of balance. You lose your sense of balance in old age. It comes on slowly, but the day arrives when you are always conscious of it. I don't at all care to be at the top of an escalator; any flight of stairs is a matter of expedient attention. In the street, curbs have become unreliable; they seem to shoot up or down unexpectedly, to vary in height, and require stern treatment. The possibility of a fall grins and glares every day; what would have been a mere indignity twenty or thirty years ago could be catastrophic now. We fall about, we old, not because we are careless but because we no longer float around with easy balance, and a fall, for many, is the prelude to incapacity. I watch rugby players and footballers with wonder, as another species. And children—that glorious pliancy, which one knew, and has forgotten.

Kingsley Amis fell over a great deal, in his later years. In his case, this would seem to have been on account of drink taken, more often than not; Martin Amis's acute memoir *Experience* wryly records heaving his father up from the road, and the overhead crashes heard by his mother, living in the flat beneath. I have fallen twice in the last five years (drink not at issue); once on the pavement near home, having apparently slipped on a squashed tomato, and once on a treacherous staircase in France ("Une chute d'escalier," I heard the ER nurse say, in a bored tone—they were shunted in daily, I suppose). I was lucky both times—no broken bones, though the staircase had my back raging for many weeks. And in neither case was balance the root cause, I think; those particular tumbles could have happened to a thirty-year-old. But both events shook me up, and made me realize that from now on any kind of fall was potentially disastrous. After seventy, stay vertical if you possibly can, is the rule.

My artist aunt, Rachel Reckitt, fell off her horse when she was eighty-two. She was a few miles from home, on the edge of the Brendons, in west Somerset, and the horse, finding himself riderless, simply did what horses do, and headed for his stable. A neighbor spotted him, a search party was organized, and found Rachel on her way down from the hill, slightly bruised and annoyed about all the fuss. After that, we persuaded her to wear a whistle when out riding. She objected strongly, and had to be reminded that this strategy had saved the day for her own elderly uncle, many years before, who had come off his horse up on Exmoor and lay for hours in a bog with a fractured leg.

Rachel died at eighty-six, working daily in her studio until her last illness. That horse survived her, the last of many she had owned, in this case an irritable pony called Fury ("A tiresome creature," she used to say, but she could no longer get up on to the big hunters she preferred). Fury himself was fifteen, which is a ripe age for a horse, and in the sad and onerous dispersal process after her death he became a central problem: nobody wanted him. Eventually, someone with field space was bribed to provide an expensive retirement.

Fury was true to form, in this; he was all set to cost. Old age costs; it costs the nation, it costs those going through it. We contribute nothing, but require maintenance—a winter fuel allowance, free TV license, bus pass, free prescriptions, all the state indulgences. Those don't add up to luxury, for anyone, any more than the state pension does other than provide basic subsistence. And old age has its needs, its greeds. You may not yearn for a Caribbean cruise—I don't—but certain comforts have become essential, the accustomed perks that make daily existence a bit more than just that. I can't start the day without a bowl of the right kind of muesli topped with some fruit and sheep's milk yogurt; I can't end it without a glass (or two) of wine. I need the diversions of radio and television. I want flowers in the house and something tempting to eat—these are greeds, I think, rather than needs. And—high priority—there is reading, the daily fix, the time of immersion in whatever is top of my book pile right now. As demands, requirements, all of this is relatively modest. Much of it—the reading, the flowers—goes back to prelapsarian days before old age. The difference, though, is that then there were further needs and greeds, and those seem to have melted away, to have tactfully absented themselves as though to make things a bit easier because they would indeed be an encumbrance now.

I am no longer acquisitive. I was never exactly voracious, but I could fall prey to sudden lust: one simply could not live a moment longer without that sampler spotted in an antique shop, or that picture or rug or chair. No longer. I can admire, but I no longer covet. Books of course are another matter; books are not acquisitions, they are necessities.

I don't need or want excitement. Pleasure, enjoyment—yes. But that restless feeling that you must have something happen, you must look ahead, anticipate, you need a rush of adrenaline—that is gone, quite gone. Thanks be. Something to look forward to—yes. Seeing family, friends. Outings—a theater, a gallery, a jaunt. Time in Somerset with Josephine. But I no longer want that dangerous edge to things—anticipation heightened by risk, the sense of adventure. I am done with adventure.

I was going to write: I am no longer aspirational. But that is not quite true. I do aspire in terms of wanting to do what I do as well as possible. I would still like to write a good book. But I don't have that ferocity for achievement that I can remember from early writing days: write a good book or bust. I have never been particularly competitive—and writers can be competitive, a trait fostered by the spectator sport of literary prizes; nowadays I find that it is other writers who are providing me with my greatest pleasures, as I pounce on a new work by Julian Barnes, Ian McEwan, Adam Thorpe, Matthew Kneale, Lawrence Norfolk, Anne Tyler, Jane Gardam, a bunch of others . . . Or as I light on one of the newer, younger writers, with the recognition that—yes, here is the sort of thing I want. I suppose that this is the reader in me taking command. But it is also, I think, a writerly satisfaction in seeing it done by others as I would wish it done—in seeing the show kept on the road. Maybe elderly athletes enjoy watching the hundred meters in the same spirit.

Out with acquisition, excitement, and aspiration except in tempered mode. And, on another front, I don't in the least lament certain emotions. I can remember falling in love, being in love; life would have been incomplete without that particular exaltation, but I wouldn't want to go back there. I still love—there is a swathe of people that I love—but I am glad indeed to be done with that consuming, tormenting form of the emotion.

So this is old age, and I am probably shedding readers by the drove at this point. If you are not yet in it, you may be shuddering. If you are, you will perhaps disagree, in which case I can only say: this is how it is for me. And if it sounds—to anyone—a pretty pallid sort of place, I can refute that. It is not.

Certain desires and drives have gone. But what remains is response. I am as alive to the world as I have ever been—alive to everything I see and hear and feel. I revel in this morning's March sunshine, and the cream and purple hellebore just out in the garden; I listen to a radio discussion about the ethics of selective abortion, and chip in at points; the sound of a beloved voice on the phone brings a surge of pleasure. Yesterday, I rejoiced in the David Hockney exhibition at the Royal Academy (for the third time)—that singing color, that exuberance (and he is seventy-five); I am reading John Lanchester's *Capital*, slowly because it is the sort of capacious novel I like and I don't want it to end. I think there is a sea change, in old age—a metamorphosis of the sensibilities. With those old consuming vigors now muted, something else comes into its own—an almost luxurious appreciation of the world that you are still in. Spring was never so vibrant; autumn never so richly gold. Maybe that's why Hockney is painting like this, now. People are of abiding interest—observed in the street, overheard on a bus. The small pleasures have bloomed into points of relish in the day—food, opening the newspaper (new minted, just for me), a shower, the comfort of bed. It is almost like some kind of end-game salute to the intensity of childhood experience, when the world was new. It is an old accustomed world now, but invested with fresh significance; I've seen all this before, done all this, but am somehow able to find new and sharpened pleasure.

On a good day, aches and pains in abeyance. On a bad day—well, on a bad day a sort of shutter comes down, and the world is dulled. But I know that it is there, the shutter will roll up, with luck, the sun will come out.

The stereotypes of old age run from the smiling old dear to the grumbling curmudgeon. In fiction, they are rife—indeed fiction is perhaps mainly responsible for the standard perception of the old, with just a few writers able to raise the game. Muriel Spark's *Memento Mori* is a black comedy, with a group of elderly plagued by sinister phone calls: "Remember you must die." No stereotypes, but a bunch of sharply drawn individuals, convincingly old, bedeviled by specific ailments, and mainly concerned with revisions of their pasts in terms of will-making and the machinations of relationships. Kingsley Amis also went for comedy, in *Ending Up*, with a group cohabiting in a cottage and busy scoring points off each other— funny, but with a bleak undertone. Saul Bellow's *Ravelstein* is neither comedy (though not without humor) nor stereotype, but strong writing about the view both of and from old age. And he was old—eighty-four—when the book was published, whereas neither Spark nor Amis were—Muriel Spark was forty-one when *Memento Mori* came out. Just three examples; they spring to mind simply because memorable and effective writing about old age is rare, though there are of course other instances. My point is that old age seems to be a danger zone for many novelists, somehow even more of a challenge than the universal problem of writing about and from the point of view of a man if you are a woman, and vice versa; we all have to deal with that unless we are to be left with a very curiously populated novel. But the old and the young are, somehow, the elusive element; equally, few novelists are good at children.

"What do they think has happened, the old fools, / To make them like this?" Any reference to Philip Larkin's poem in this context is almost a cliché. The poem marries perception of age with stark truth: "Well, / We shall find out." He never did, of course, dying at sixty-three. And the perception is of drooling, confused, incapable old age—not a stereotype so much as an evocation, both harsh and reflective.

Those of us not yet in the departure lounge and still able to take a good look at what has made them—us—like this can find some solace in doing so. What has happened is such an eccentric mixture of immediate and long-drawn-out, the arrival of a condition that has been decades in the making but seems to have turned up this morning. The succession of people that we have been— Sir Thomas Browne's "varieties of himself"— are suddenly elided into this—final?—version, disturbingly alien when we catch sight of a mirror, but also evocative of a whole range of known personae. What we have been still lurks—and even more so within. This old-age self is just a top dressing, it seems; early selves are still mutinously present, getting a word in now and then. And all this is interesting—hence the solace. I never imagined that old age would be quite like this—possibly because, like most, I never much bothered to imagine it.

My attitude towards these earlier selves— varieties of myself—is peculiar, I find. It is kindly, indulgent—as though towards a younger relative, sometimes impatient (you idiot . . .), occasionally grateful. I'm grateful for all that work done—a bunch of other people wrote my books, it can seem. I feel kindly towards those recognizable former incarnations, in whom I can see my present self— reading Sir Thomas Browne in the 1970s, digging our first garden in Swansea in 1961, entranced when my first baby laughs—spring of 1958. I'm angry about the mistakes, the deficiencies, the times I should have done differently.

This book is to be about the context of a lifetime. Some of this context lies within my own head—the shape-shifting backdrop of memory. There is a rich population here, all those people in the mind, my own previous selves, and alongside them so many others—transient encounters and, most vividly, family and friends.

My old-age friends go back a long way. Twenty years, thirty, sixty—Susan and I were twenty together—and even seventy-five years, two were known in my Egyptian childhood. And now here we are sharing this new incarnation. Or is it new? Because they all seem to me much as they ever were. We behave toward each other much the same, except that we inquire after health in a way that we never used to—really wanting to know, not that casual perfunctory "How *are* you?" But, I suppose because we have kept up with one another all along the way, we are not taken aback by the metamorphosis, the way we look now. When I was on the other side of the Atlantic a few years ago staying with my best friend in America, she produced a photo she had found of the two of us taken in the early 1980s. We gazed at it with surprised respect; "Weren't we young!" said Betty. Actually, verging on middle age, but never mind—our reaction was in perfect accord: an acknowledgment of those other selves. Steve, next-door neighbor of my childhood, seems remote today from the six-year-old in my head, with whom I am still playing a messy game by the garden pond involving ships made of pieces of plank, but there is a resonance. He became a sculptor, and back then he was in charge of plank construction: talent will out. I go back thirty years and more with Ann and Anthony; they are layered in my head, saying and doing over time, a collective with a concertina effect that compresses to the known people of today. Several decades again with Joy, and it is sometimes a familiar younger self of hers who surfaces—a turn of phrase, a mannerism.

And others . . . The point of all this is a tribute to the way in which we are each of us the accretion of all that we have been. You see this in yourself; you see it in those you have long known. Nothing new here, no fresh perception, but something you appreciate to the full in old age. I am aware of invisible ballast, on all sides, the hidden body of the iceberg.

I cherish the company of my contemporaries, but I want—need—also to touch base elsewhere. Two of my closest friends today are considerably younger than I am, and I value that; the great stimulus over the last twenty years has been watching, and knowing, my grandchildren, four of them now grown up. To be corralled with one's own age group must seem like some kind of malign exile, a banishment from the rich every-age confection of society. To walk along the street and see a toddler in a stroller, a bunch of teenagers, businesspeople on their cell phones, middle-aged women with their shopping, someone else elderly like me, is to feel a part of the natural progression of things, to be aware of continuity, replenishment. And it is, quite simply, of consuming interest; a novelist is anyway a people-watcher—an old novelist is still in the business but in less forensic style. There is a kind of benign observation now; the street scene mutates from season to season, year to year. New adornment; different style. How on earth does she get into those skin-tight jeans? Tattoos *all* over *both* arms—you may get tired of that, you know. *Three* matching pugs with matching collars and leashes?

We old are on the edge of things. Or are we? Yesterday was budget day, and the airwaves are full of outrage at the so-called "granny tax"—the phasing out of tax concessions for those over sixty-five. Unfair to penalize those who have worked and saved, is the cry, but there is also threatening mention of the "gray vote." We might bite back. No doubt all this has been taken into consideration by those whose job it is to crunch the numbers, but the fact remains that there is an uneasy tension today between proper concern for the old, and a nervous apprehension about this exponential growth of a new demographic. We are many, and will be more; on the edge, perhaps, but unignorable.

The day belongs to the young, the younger. I feel overtaken, and that is fine. I don't like finding myself usually the oldest person in the room, and I am afraid of being boring. The old carry around the potential to bore like a red warning light; I know, I have shied away from it myself. But I wouldn't in the least want to reoccupy the center stage, which is I suppose that midlife period around forty, with youth still apparent and middle age at arm's length. I don't remember being any more appreciative of life then than I am now. More energy, yes, of course—vigor, capacity—but plenty of doubts and anxieties. Well, there still are those, but tempered somehow by experience; you don't fret or waver less, but you have learned that time will sort it out, for better or for worse.

Experience. What is it? The employer's question: "What is your experience?" Mere existence is experience; being here, exposed, involved, no choice in the matter, get on and make what you can of it. At eighty, you have a war chest of experience—euphoric, appalling, good, bad, indifferent. You may have learned from it: The stark truth is that you know rather more than you did at twenty. Or at thirty, or forty. But don't go on about that; they will find out for themselves.

We old talk too much about the past; this should take place only between consenting contemporaries. Boredom hovers, for others—unless by special request for purposes of information or instruction. We must beware that glassy smile of polite attention: they are searching for an exit strategy. Fold up the past and put it away— available for private study. This is now, and while still present and a part of it, we do best to remember that that is where we are. This may sound a touch brutal; it is simply that I have become conscious of the need—for me, at least— to stay tuned in. Memory is crucial, memory is everything, but to retreat there would be a fatal detachment.

Memory is the subject for another section—the crutch, the albatross, the defining story, all the things that it is for any of us. I remember (see?) getting interested first in the operation of memory when in my forties—midlife, or thereabouts. Today, old, I am conscious of it as definition (shadow of the dreaded dementia) and, above all, as that essential setting. What has happened to me, but also what has happened while I have been around, which is where I go next—an examination of my own historical context both as it seemed at the time and how it seems now, with the wisdoms of analysis by others.

Life and Times

I was a wartime child. There were millions of us, and for many the experience was hideous. I was growing up in Egypt, where I was born. For me, the Libyan desert campaign of the early 1940s was simply the state of the world, the way things were; it sent us for a while to Palestine, then it receded, vanished. War continued, of course, but more distantly; it rumbled on, it was a condition, no more and no less.

Children do not question their circumstances. You are you, in this place, at this time, with these people—how could it be otherwise? I was required to say my prayers, every night: "Please God, help me to be a good girl, and make the war end soon." A mantra repeated without interest or conviction. War was a word; it was language, first and foremost, language that swirled around me, above my head, language that did indeed create the times, the place, that has lodged, that can still—just—turn then into now.

Tobruk. Benghazi. Mersa Matruh. Alamein. Monty. The Auk. Churchill.

Before the war. After the war. For the duration. Peacetime. Shrapnel. Destroyers. Depth charges.

67

Searchlights. Battledress. Armored cars. Jeeps. Tanks.

Spitfires. Hurricanes.

War was The War—this single commanding inescapable fact that so occupied grown-ups. It was constant, like the Egyptian sun. It was there, as far as I was concerned—as abiding as sunshine, as unremarkable.

"I have to tell you that no such undertaking has been received and consequently this country is at war with Germany": I know those words because I have heard and read them many times. But I heard them first when I was six—a thin, dry voice coming from the wireless in my grandmother's drawing room in Somerset, 3 September 1939. They were language that I did not understand, and to which I did not listen; I had been told that I must sit still and keep quiet, this required all my attention. But The War had stalked into the room, and into my life. It would shortly send me on a helter-skelter journey down through Europe, clutching a gas mask which I must not lose (why? what is it, anyway?), back across the Mediterranean to Cairo, home, and the garden that was the haven of my childhood, with its eucalyptus and casuarina trees, its poinsettias and lantana, zinnias and plumbago, the banyan, the bamboo, the bougainvillea, the arum lilies. More language, defining language, language that provides a child with that other crucial dimension—what you see is expanded into what you hear.

I am trying to see *then* against the wisdoms of *now,* to look at the climactic points of the last century, to fish out what it felt like to be around at that point, if possible, and set that against the long view, the story now told, the arguments and the verdicts.

The experience of childhood presents the greatest challenge. It is in one sense crystal clear, in another sense irretrievable. It is the smell of crushed eucalyptus leaves, the crash of waves against the stone rampart of the Corniche in Alexandria, the shrapnel trophy gathered at an air raid there, the cool grip on my finger of the chameleon I have found in the garden. But it is also gone, it cannot be recovered. It is swamped, drowned out by adult knowledge. That child self is an alien; I have still some glimmer of what she saw, but her mind is unreachable: I know too much, seventy years on.

That war—The War—is packed away into books, and I read with fascination. It is history now, and not packed tidily, laid to rest, because there is nothing tidy or restful about history. The battle of Alamein has been differently fought, decade by decade. Did Montgomery simply take over plans originated by Auchinleck? Had Auchinleck intended a withdrawal of the Eighth Army to Khartoum and Palestine, if need be? The subsequent analyses chew over reputations, strategies, who said what to whom, why this happened, why that did not. Language illuminates, once more: "I am fighting a terrific battle with Rommel," writes Montgomery, sidelining a few hundred thousand others, ". . . a terrific party and a complete slogging match." And, for me, I hear again the Cairo chatter of 1942: so-and-so is in the bag, someone else bought it when his tank brewed up.

The battle—or battles, depending on the analysis—of Alamein turned the tide of the desert war and stopped Rommel's advance into Egypt; that much is generally agreed. If it had not—well, at the most extreme estimate, the entire course of the war might have run differently, and possibly disastrously for the Allies. The Axis forces could have swept up through Palestine into Syria, Iran, Iraq, the oilfields there that must have been Hitler's target. If it had not—at a purely personal level, we would have lost our home, and my father, who stayed in Cairo when my mother and I went to Palestine along with other British women and children as Rommel advanced, would have been interned. It was said that our house a few miles outside Cairo had been earmarked for Rommel's retreat. So it would have been the German commander and his staff officers sipping gin and tonic on the veranda of an evening, instead of my parents and their friends, and diving into the large, raised concrete tank that was grandly called our swimming pool, and fraternizing with our dog, which was, conveniently, a dachshund.

I have written elsewhere of those years, of how it seemed to a nine/ten-year-old. I can still see it thus—eyes screwed up, peering backward—but the effect is refracted now by time and discussion. The language that was once normal seems archaic; the clipped upper-class diction of the day startles me—the voices of news bulletins, of old films—can that really once have been familiar? The background clamor of the Libyan campaign—the army convoys on the desert road to Alexandria, the searchlight battery in the fields near our house, the soldiers on the streets of Cairo, the talk of the next big push—is reduced now to the cold print of the books on my shelves. I can read about what happened; about what they say happened.

Keith Douglas, soldier poet who fought at Alamein and was killed in Normandy, aged twenty-four, wrote his memoir *Alamein to Zem Zem* soon after the campaign, probably in 1943: "I observed these battles partly as an exhibition— that is to say that I went through them like a visitor from the country, going to a great show, or like a child in a factory—a child sees the brightness and efficiency of steel machines and endless belts slapping round and round, without caring what it is all for . . . The dates have slipped away, the tactical lessons have been learnt by someone else . . . Against a backcloth of indeterminate landscapes, of moods and smells, dance the black and bright incidents." And he makes them dance in that brief and vivid memoir, which is furnished with his own arresting, dashed-off sketches: the contorted corpse of a Libyan soldier, a tank crew cooking on a sand-filled petrol can. He gives the view from a tank (he was a tank commander, at twenty-one, fresh out from England, after a few months' training in the Delta), like that in a silent film, since the noise of the engine drowns out all other sounds, he gives the camaraderie and irritation of the officers' mess, he gives fear and exhilaration and the abiding, impervious presence of the western desert. It is a masterly piece of writing; when I reread it, I think with wonder that this life, his life, all those lives, were running thus just a hundred miles or so from where my child self was in animistic communion with the eucalyptus tree in our garden, or reading *Tales from Greece and Rome* under the banyan, or surfing the glorious waves of Sidi Bishr, in Alexandria. Seventy years on, that young man seems locked into that time, smiling out from the photo in the memoir, khaki-clad, moustached, looking rather older than he actually was. I read his poetry as a message from another world. There should have been more of it.

Wartime Cairo steamed with poets. Bernard

Spencer, Robin Fedden, Terence Tiller, John Gawsworth, John Cromer, Gwyn Williams, Robert Liddell—none of these names would be familiar today to anyone outside the arcane world of mid-twentieth-century poetry studies. G. S. Fraser, a leading light, did have a postwar role as a prominent figure in London literary life; Tiller worked for the BBC and produced a radio adaptation of *Lord of the Rings*. Lawrence Durrell is known now as a novelist, for *The Alexandria Quartet*, but was working mainly as a poet in the early 1940s, and was one of the Alexandria gang of poets, with Robert Liddell and Gwyn Williams, exchanging insults and jokes with the Cairo crowd—Fedden, Spencer, Tiller. Keith Douglas was published in *Personal Landscape*, the literary magazine launched by Spencer and Tiller, and can fairly be said to be the only one of those wartime Cairo poets regarded today as a significant voice of the Second World War.

All were young—very young—as was most of the febrile, hectic Cairo society of those years, marvelously described in Artemis Cooper's *Cairo in the War*. Parties, drinks on the terrace at Shepheard's, drinks by the pool at the Gezira Sporting Club, more parties, expeditions to Luxor, to the Fayoum, yet another party. The Eighth Army officer buccaneers were at the heart of it; they came and went, and some went entirely—in the bag, or bought it. There were various planes of society—the Embassy circle, the bankers, the cotton magnates, the British Council, the universities—coteries and groupings but plenty of overlap in an overcrowded, centralized city. Lawrence Durrell was foreign press attaché at the British Embassy, so with a foot in that camp as well as the more informal world of the Anglo-Egyptian Union and the Victory Club. Robin Fedden was a lecturer at Fuad al Awad University; I remember him at my mother's lunch parties, and that he taught our cook to make a dish I hated involving highly spiced lamb, apricots, nuts and garlic. Our cuisine was sternly English (rice pudding, cottage pie) and this injection of what sounds like pure Claudia Roden, and very good too, affronted me—the only brush with the esoteric world of the Cairo poets of which I am aware.

I came to England in a troopship in early April 1945; seven thousand demobilized soldiers and a hundred expatriate women and children, going home. Except for me, who was leaving home. It was a transition from the Middle Eastern world of warmth and color to the chill gray of England, and wartime England at that, with its own hectoring vocabulary of coupons and points and identity cards and shortages. The war was not yet over; the V2 rocket offensive in London had reached a new intensity in February, the last weapon did not fall until the end of March. It was not until May 7 that the war officially ended, and the VE Day crowds surged through central London, dancing, singing, a sea of faces in front of Buckingham Palace, Churchill up there on the balcony with the royal family, flourishing V sign and cigar.

No, I did not see that. Reaching back for that summer, all I can find is an array of personal concerns, the problems of a traumatized teenager uprooted from what had seemed a homeland, whose parents had just divorced, and who had now ended up in an alien society where the social codes were mysterious and the climate defied belief. I was so cold. Well, so were most, back then, with coal the equivalent of black gold and central heating a concept of the future. Forget dancing in the streets; I was being outfitted for my first school, a dire establishment on the south coast. I met Chilprufe vests for the first time, and liberty bodices, and navy wool knickers. The war might have ended, but another had begun, for me.

But there is a landscape, in my mind—the eloquent landscape of London in 1945: the city fingered by the blitz, then again by the V1s and the V2s. I did surface enough from my own distresses to notice that: the houses with gaping façades, the floors gone, the ghost of a staircase snaking up, a fireplace clinging to a wall, the shape of a picture or mirror. The sudden absence in a street, like a tooth socket, a space filled with rubble and weeds. Someone took me to see the annihilation at the heart of the City; whenever now I come across that iconic photo of St Paul's rising above the wasteland I have my own clear, complementary vision—the acreage of low walls fringing lakes of purple willow-herb, the cathedral enormous, startling, restored to its original dominance, everything else shorn to the ground. The willow-herb rampaged, birds sang.

My artist aunt, Rachel Reckitt, was in London throughout the blitz of 1941 and 1942, working at Toynbee Hall in Stepney, where she was one of those helping to organize the evacuation of women and children. Whenever she could, she made sketches of the bomb-blasted city, sketches that she would later—much later, in some cases—use as the basis for oil paintings and for the wood engravings for which she is distinguished. These hang on my walls today, and I look at them constantly. London of today is reminded of London then: *House in Fulham*, in which the shattered building serves as backdrop to a great pile of rubble from which, at the base, peers a Union Jack; *House in Berkeley Square*, three tiers of exposed doors, fireplaces, patches of wallpaper. And *Demolition*, where men with sacking hoods shift basket-loads of rubble; jagged walls, a fallen ladder, a flight of steps that go nowhere. The subject matter has become a display of the engraver's craft: the minuscule hatching and crosshatching, the intensity of detail that becomes a kind of patterning, the subtle shadings to darkest black, the flares of white light. These are master-pieces of engraving; you study them for the intricacy, the effect. But they are also works of art about something once observed; she had sat sketching, back then, in front of a scene like this—that smashed house, those striving demolition workers. The engravings remember.

As do I. Such sights were commonplace, you did not much stop and stare. The demolition men were gone, but the scarred landscape was there. I did not wonder at it, particularly; it was just another strange feature of this foreign world in which I found myself. The war had been here too, as in Egypt, if differently. I took note, but my immediate concerns were offensive underwear, and how to conform with new requirements. London had an etiquette, it seemed; I was no longer a child, they told me, I must wear gloves and lisle stockings, learn the procedures of the day. This was the class-ridden society of the midcentury; people were defined by speech and dress. I too must be defined, and understand the definitions. For one who had grown up amid the cosmopolitan exuberance of Cairo these were indistinct and baffling. Londoners all looked and sounded the same to me.

I can sympathize with that, inspecting photos of street scenes of back then: the housewives, uniformed in coat to just below the knee, felt hat on head. All women seem to wear hats—they indicate neither age nor class; most men wear raincoats. But all, now, are lodged in an unfamiliar past; I don't recognize them as people who must once have furnished the world I knew. Along with wartime idioms, and the clipped speech of the day.

Does anyone identify with the age in which they were young? I don't. It seems to me more that we slide accommodatingly along with the decades, adjusting plumage as we go—dressing accordingly, thinking accordingly, or up to a point. I don't feel out of sympathy with today, by no means, though it has aspects that I deplore; I can play the grumpy old woman at moments. But there is far more that is alien and unappealing about 1945. And if I were again to feel nostalgic for polyglot and cosmopolitan Cairo—well, I have only to get out into London of today. A stroll round my own area this morning, and I hear Russian, Chinese, French, an eastern European language I cannot identify, ditto African. As for neutrality of dress, or being able to tell what sort of a person you are looking at—forget it. There are dress codes, yes—the urban hoodie, young fashionistas—but by and large I can have very little idea of a person from their dress or how they speak.

I am a Londoner now, of many years standing. I am not sure that I love London—countryside feels more like home—but I am acclimatized. I can appreciate organic London, the metamorphosis of a city, the shape-changing city, the way in which it moves with time. That is what I most like about London—its eloquence, long story, the sense in which it is of the moment, this year, these mores, but is also a permanence, a solidity that outlives the racy window-dressing of new bars, new restaurants, new shops, new talk, new ways of living, a different layer of people.

Some windows of my house in an Islington square have early glass—that beguiling, irregular glass beyond which trees ripple and change shape, a passing aircraft quivers and dissolves. These windows must have survived the blitz; indeed, the square appears to be unscathed, but the London Bomb Damage map for the area makes a silent comment: one house, a few doors from mine, is colored dark red—Seriously Damaged, Doubtful if Repairable. A direct hit, presumably, but the building seems to have been put together again. These fascinating and eloquent maps show the city, street by street and house by house, with the color coding that plots the extent of damage, from Total Destruction to Blast Damage, Minor in Nature. Large and small circles pinpoint the strike of a V1 or a V2. Islington is liberally picked out in every color—black, purple, dark red, light red, orange, yellow—each neat coloring-in of a house or street remembering some night of carnage, the maps becoming a strange and rather beautiful testimony. Much of Islington is early Victorian, houses that are a thin skin of brick. They always seem to me, now, to be holding each other up. Beneath the bombs, an entire street could go down like ninepins. My own house must have shuddered under the blast of that bomb a few doors away; the bricks remember. A few hundred yards away a land mine fell on the corner of Ritchie Street, obliterating a large site, now rebuilt. The whole borough is pockmarked like this, the post war new builds inserted into the Victorian infrastructure, replacing the rubble and the willowherb. Islington knew the V2s; a pub on the corner of Mackenzie Road and Holloway Road was flattened on Boxing Day 1944, along with twenty houses and shop premises: seventy-one dead and fifty-six seriously injured. Another Islington rocket on January 13, 1945, killed twenty-nine and seriously injured thirty-six.

So the blitz has a legacy; it is still here, its manipulation of the city is visible, as though a giant hand swept through the place, knocking this down, plucking that out. And then other hands rebuilt, steadily, doggedly, just as they always have done, century by century, the place reinventing itself, expanding, responding to new requirements, new populations. And the real blitz, the actual thing, the *Sturm und Drang*, has slipped off into history, into the books, into the documentaries and the fictional reconstructions. It has spun its own legends of chirpy Cockney courage, of the King and Queen picking their way through the ruins of the East End, of heroism and stoicism. And the darker stories of those who seized the day: the black-marketeers, the looters who kept people camping out in their bomb-damaged homes in case they lost everything, the opportunists who snatched rings and watches from the bodies of those killed in the Piccadilly Café de Paris bombing.

My aunt Rachel, on the front line as it were, recorded her own vision in letters to her mother—brisk, factual letters that reflect her own vigor and energy (she was thirty-two at the time). She was giving an account of what she saw and did, of the behavior of those with whom she was dealing (September 1940): "It was exciting starting out this morning to view the damage. The first I saw was the Science Museum, all the large towers still standing, but the centre all gone. Up in Central London there was a big fire in Holborn, and various small craters to see, and then a big crater bang in the middle of the roadway between the Bank, Royal Exchange and a public shelter. It couldn't have missed more important targets if it had tried! . . . The people . . . really are wonderful. Lots were wandering, homeless, towards the City this morning, with suitcases, all they had saved, but they seemed quite resigned and unmoved . . .

None of the homeless people I had in were grumbling; they were all determined we must stick it out . . . There seems to be only one billeting officer for refugees, so, naturally, he can never be got hold of by anyone; no canteens seem to function and of course all the gas, etc., is off, so people can't get hot food. They are still sticking it wonderfully well . . . I can have up to £30 to use for travelling expenses of intending evacuees who have an address to go to and don't come under any scheme. So I have got one or two off today in this way. Generally when they ask to be evacuated I ask, 'Has your house been demolished yet?' and if it hasn't I have to tell them to wait until it has, as then we can do something. So later they come in with broad grins to announce that now it has been blown up and they can get away . . . There was an exciting air battle today—a big lot of Germans ran into a barrage of AA fire, one could see them scatter and rock in it, all very high up. Then they met our fighters, but came right over us so we had to stop watching. The sky seemed full of them for a few minutes. They came in the evening to drop incendiaries to start fires to guide them later . . . there is no evacuation scheme for old people, the blind, cripples, etc., who are too infirm to get to the shelters and have to lie and wait to be bombed. They don't matter so much as the children, of course, but something might be done . . . The *Evening Standard* carried a front page article on how the old and infirm are able to be evacuated, but are not availing themselves of the opportunity. It is cruel as of course it is entirely untrue and merely raises their hopes. The poor old things are dying to go in hundreds of cases."

"Exciting . . ." she says, more than once. And I imagine that in an eerie way it was, to a young woman whose life hitherto had been led in the rural tranquility of west Somerset. The experience affected her deeply; not only did it provoke an artistic response, but the revelation of urban poverty turned her into a lifelong socialist. She voted Labour thereafter, to the bewilderment of my grandmother, an entrenched conservative.

The blitz—the war in general—has taken on a sepia quality today, and, indeed, a sense of romance has taken hold. You don't get any fictional slant on the 1940s—on the page or onscreen—in which young love does not take center stage. For many, those years probably did have that flavor; certainly, hasty wartime marriages were a feature. I was the wrong age for the war, I realize; a child is a bystander. Ten years older, and you stood a good chance of getting killed, or you might have the time of your life.

By 1945 I was no longer a child, perched now on that perilous interface between childhood and adult life. There weren't teenagers back then; the status had not been invented. We were apprentice adults, very much on sufferance; our clothes were bought to last, we must not smoke or drink or go to restricted-films, we must behave ourselves and mark time until admitted to the real world. Most of us left school at fifteen, and were pitched into adult work; relatively few made their way into the privileged holding-pen of student life.

My university years seem to me now to have been lived in a sort of mindless trance. Not in an academic sense—I was reading history, and I know that those reading years have colored my thinking ever since—but in absence of response to what was going on in the world. This was the early 1950s; plenty was going on, but it was not a time of student activism. Membership of the Oxford Union—the student debating society— was open to men only; those with political ambitions spoke there, and jockeyed for office. I have a vague memory of Michael Heseltine, a youth with floppy golden hair, and impeccably cut suits at a period when most male students wore gray flannels and duffel coats. I must have voted for the first time, but I don't remember the event.

The autumn of 1956 woke me up. The Suez crisis. I was in Oxford still, working as research assistant by then to a Fellow of St. Antony's College. St. Antony's was—is—a graduate college, specializing then in Middle Eastern and Soviet studies. It was international, a hotbed of young intellectuals. The group with which I became friendly included Americans, a Frenchman, an

Israeli, a German, and Jack Lively, from Newcastle, my soon-to-be husband, who had come over from Cambridge to a research fellowship at the college. The unfolding drama of Suez, and the growing possibility of British/French intervention after Nasser's nationalization of the Canal, polarized opinion throughout the country; Oxford was in a ferment of discussion, with those opposed to Prime Minister Anthony Eden's increasingly belligerent stance in a majority. Jack, along with a colleague at St. Antony's, set about a campaign to coordinate a response by senior members of the university, immediately after the first bombing raids on Cairo. I remember cycling round from college to college delivering personal letters summoning sympathizers to a meeting at which a statement was drafted, signed by three hundred and fifty-five members of Senior Common Rooms and ten heads of colleges, led by Alan Bullock of St. Catherine's. The statement read: "We consider that this action is morally wrong, that it endangers the solidarity of the Commonwealth, that it constitutes a grave strain on the Atlantic Alliance and that it is a flagrant violation of the UN charter." I couldn't be at the meeting, not being a senior member of the university, but I remember vividly the heightened atmosphere of that time, the urgency of the newspapers, the climate of discussion, of argument, and eventually, for many of us, of outrage.

For me, what was happening had a personal dimension—here was my own country dropping bombs on the country I still thought of as a kind of home. The Suez crisis was a baptism of fire, a political awakening, the recognition that you could and should quarrel with government, that you could disagree and disapprove.

Over half a century ago now, Suez, and nicely consigned to history: my granddaughter Izzy "did" it for her A level. I too can read about it, and set what I read against what is in my head still—those autumn days in Oxford, when the talk was all of the names now packed away into the books: Eisenhower, Dulles, Ben-Gurion, Hammarskjöld, Gaitskell, Bevan. And, dominating all, Eden and Nasser. There was a sequence of events—dismaying, startling, often inexplicable events—and plenty of judgments, applause, condemnations, warnings. History has tidied it all up, to some extent—what happened when, and why, the inexplicable is explained. The judgments of history are of course equally various, but one thing does seem clear: there are not many today who defend Britain's—Eden's—handling of the Suez crisis. Peter Hennessy has written: "It is rare to be able to claim, historically, that but for one person, the course of history would almost entirely have been different. In the case of Suez, one can."

On July 26, 1956, Gamal Abdel Nasser, president

of Egypt, declared Egypt's nationalization of the Suez Canal, seizing control of the Suez Canal Company and proclaiming military law in the Canal Zone. Since the conception of the Canal by the French diplomat Ferdinand de Lesseps, its construction under his aegis, and its opening in 1869, it had been administered under largely French management but with Britain owning forty-four percent of the Company's shares. The Company never owned the Canal; it owned the concession to operate this crucial waterway that was on Egyptian territory, a waterway that united the Mediterranean and the Red Sea, vital to international shipping—the passage to India, to southern Africa, to the Far East.

There was a background to Nasser's action. He was angered by the withdrawal of the Anglo-American aid offer for his Aswan Dam project; Eden had initially favored this, anxious to preempt Soviet influence with Nasser, and in the Middle East generally, but his attitude toward Nasser had hardened, as he came to see him as an enemy of the West. Eden acceded to U.S. withdrawal from patronage of the Aswan Dam. Nasser reacted immediately and conclusively in the one way that he could, by taking over the Canal. Egypt's Canal would be managed by Egyptians—a step that vastly increased his popularity at home but challenged the West.

Over the Suez crisis lay the shadow of the Cold

War. There was always the fear that Russia would make a move—exploit the situation to exert control over Middle Eastern oil supplies; it is always about oil, then as now—Suez, Iraq—the bulk of European oil supplies came through the Canal in the midcentury. And, more local and immediate, the simmering hostility between Israel and her Arab neighbors. The complexities of the situation have fattened the history books; to distill the international commotion of 1956 into a simple narrative is to leave out most of the surrounding clamor, but I am not writing history—I am trying to sort out what I now know happened and think of it against what seemed at the time to be happening. Now, I have all the advantages of hindsight, and the wisdoms of Peter Hennessy, Keith Kyle and others who have considered 1956 and drawn conclusions. Then, I was a twenty-three-year-old who, thanks to higher education but what now seems a deficient interest in current affairs, knew perhaps more about certain historic periods than what was going on in her own world. The Cold War was a term, merely; I would become more alert to that, grimly alert. The United Nations was a concept, and a good thing, but I was barely aware of it. I had never much listened to the battle cries of politicians, the cut and thrust of the House of Commons. That October, I paid attention, and about time too.

So, what happened then, shorn of surrounding

clamor? Immediately after Nasser's seizing of the Canal on October 26 Eden set up a cabinet committee—the Egypt Committee—to oversee the crisis. Its aims were uncompromising: to get rid of Nasser and see the Canal entrusted to international management. The expression "regime change" was not yet around, but Iraq must spring to mind. With a colossal difference: Nasser was—in Eden's eyes at least—a threat to the West, but he was no Saddam Hussein. He was not a vicious tyrant; Egypt's skirmishes with Israel did not compare with the invasion of Kuwait. Nasser had laid hands on what was seen as a Franco-British asset; his action might jeopardize the West's oil supplies. And Eden had become paranoid about him.

The next weeks and months saw the clandestine maneuvring that has become, in retrospect, the most significant feature of the Suez crisis: the Sèvres Protocol. This, in a nutshell, was a secret agreement between Britain, France, and Israel by which Israel would invade the Sinai peninsula—Egyptian territory—whereupon British and French troops would intervene under the guise of peacekeeping, and thus occupy the Canal Zone. The details, and the agreement, were hammered out at a meeting hosted by the French in a Parisian suburban villa that had once been a safe house for the Resistance; the leading participants were Guy Mollet, the French prime minister, Israel's leader Ben-Gurion, and British foreign secretary Selwyn Lloyd, who seemed both at the time and subsequently to have wished he wasn't there. The Israelis were persuaded of their role as the pretext for intervention; the Franco-British objectives were clear—destroy the Egyptian army, bring down Nasser, and occupy the Canal.

The British Cabinet was never informed about the Sèvres meeting; only a few of Eden's associates were in the know, the foreign secretary's presence was to be hushed up in perpetuity, any record was suppressed where possible. We know about it all now because there were records, people have talked. At the time, as things rushed ahead in October, unfolding precisely according to the Sèvres agreement, there were some suspicions. But only now has the great collusion become the essential—and shameful—aspect of the Suez crisis.

On October 29 Israeli paratroopers were dropped into Sinai twenty miles east of Suez, and a light division began to move in order to join up with them. At the same time an Anglo-French convoy with warships and supporting craft set sail for Port Said. On October 31 the first British bombs fell on airfields around Cairo, the idea being to neutralize or disperse the Egyptian air force so that it would not be a threat to the Israelis—which was what was done. By now, the United Nations was taking an active interest and calling for a cease-fire between Egypt and Israel—Egyptian forces were resisting in Sinai. On November 5 the British Cabinet decided that a cease-fire had not been achieved and that therefore occupation of the Canal Zone should take place. On November 6 there were seaborne landings of British tanks and commandos. Fighting took place; seven hundred and fifty to one thousand Egyptians are thought to have died, British and French killed amounted to twenty-three. And then, later on the 6th, in response to the United Nations and to American pressure, Britain and France agreed to stop their action.

It was all very quick—a few days. There had of course been weeks of preparation; the stationing of the seaborne force in Malta and Cyprus, the devising of an elaborate campaign of advance, *Musketeer*. Much of this had been all too apparent; you don't move aircraft carriers and cruisers around the Mediterranean without someone noticing, in particular the American Sixth Fleet, which had been acting as an interested shadow, and reminder of Eisenhower's displeasure at what was apparently brewing. But, when it all happened, it was done within a week—a week of newspaper headlines, mass protest meetings, furious exchanges in the House of Commons, argument in households up and down the land. Was this Britain standing up for our rights or an outrageous and illegal exercise of power?

For me, it was certainly outrageous, and also disturbingly evocative. The place-names—Suez, Ismailia, Qantara, Port Said. I had never been to Suez, which is the southernmost point of the Canal, where it joins the Red Sea. But Port Said was entirely familiar; the bustling harbor, presided over by the statue of de Lesseps. There, not that long ago, just over ten years earlier, I had stood on the deck of HMS *Ranchi* as the ship sailed past the statue, and had thought in a rather self-consciously grown-up way that this was the end of something. I was leaving Egypt forever. The year 1956 was to be the end for de Lesseps: on December 24 the statue was blown off its plinth to the jeers of an angry crowd; apparently only his shoes remain, embedded in the concrete. As for Ismailia and Qantara, both were part of my childhood, the points at which you crossed the Canal when going to Palestine, whether by train or by car, in which case the car was driven on to a ferry, an exciting and hazardous process. At Ismailia my mother had had a quarrel with an Egyptian customs official over two Palestinian tortoises I was importing in a shoebox: contraband, according to him. At Qantara I had inadvertently dropped my sandwich lunch into the Canal, leaning too far over the rail of the ferry. I knew the Canal; it was part of the landscape of the mind—a great reach of water, ships, the dockside commotion of shouting porters, people selling oranges and fizzy drinks, skulking pi-dogs, little boys begging for baksheesh. And here it was today the center of world attention and, right now, apparently, out of action entirely, blocked by wrecks the Egyptians had sunk to that end.

In April 1957 the Canal reopened, under Egyptian management. The Suez crisis was over, except of course for the repercussions. It was a long time before Anglo-American relations recovered; for some, the crisis marked the end of Britain as a Great Power. Eden resigned in January 1957 (though he lived for another twenty years). The truth was that he had been ill throughout the crisis, following a gall-bladder operation some while earlier, and was heavily dependent on medication. It does seem that his condition may have had some effect on his state of mind, and his actions, during the crucial months of 1956. Certainly a number of his associates were surprised by his responses, their bewilderment expressed in their language at the time: "gone bananas," "bonkers." His reputation never recovered—a tragedy for a man who had been a politician of integrity and a distinguished foreign secretary.

The Senior Common Rooms of Oxford settled back to more parochial matters of disagreement, except perhaps for St. Antony's, which had always been concerned with the wider world. Jack and I got married; his fellowship came to an end, we were expecting a baby, there were not many jobs around for young academics. In retrospect, we seem to have been extraordinarily unworried—no money, our home a two-room rented flat. As it was, Jack got a job—a lectureship at the University of Swansea—we moved to Wales and the next stage in life began.

In November 2006, a conference took place at the School of Oriental and African Studies: "Fifty years since Suez: from conflict to collaboration." There were British and Egyptian contributors, papers were read on political and economic relations and on cultural relations—the section to which I was asked to contribute. I talked about "cultural confusion," about what it had been like to grow up knowing myself to be English, but identifying with Egypt, and feeling an alien when eventually I arrived in my own country. And I spoke also of my feelings at the time of the Suez crisis, about my sense of outrage at what my country was doing to the country with which I still identified, about the way in which the crisis made so many of us young sit up and take notice of a political climate. I felt rather out of place amid some distinguished academics and commentators, and was surprised to be warmly received—rapturously, indeed, in some quarters. Middle-aged Egyptian men came up afterwards, putting an arm round my shoulders, fixing me with those liquid, emotional brown eyes: "Oh, Mrs. Lively, you spoke to my heart!" I basked in brief undeserved glory, and went home thinking of how then had folded into now, the clamor of 1956 distilled into analysis and opinion—and my twenty-three-year-old self become an elderly woman whose mind she still tenuously inhabited.

Suez did not so much politicize me as join me to the times. Before that, I had not been paying attention—did not much read newspapers, was blithely cruising in a solipsistic world of my own. Plenty of the young do this; public affairs are not their concern, leave that to the oldies. At the other end of life, I look back at myself with surprise, and a certain impatience. How *young*. How—not innocent, but ignorant. And how judgmental I am being now, groomed by decades of newsprint, radio, television. We are indeed in, or of, the world, there's no escaping it, why should there not be a time of prelapsarian freedom?

Because I wouldn't want it now, I suppose I am saying. I can't do without the world. And perhaps that need is a characteristic particularly of later years. I want to know—must know—what the world is up to for as long as I am still a part of it, I feel—unsettled—without one ear cocked to the clamor of events. Wake up to the *Today* program, on–off attention to that for an hour or so, read the paper, check in at one o'clock for the news, again at six, probably, and of course the television on at ten, before bed. Some of this was caught perhaps from Jack, for whom foreign travel was a torment unless he could lay hands on an English news-paper. But he was extremely concerned with politics; it was print he was mostly after—analysis and comment. For me, it is the narrative—the many narratives—the sense of an unstoppable progress, the march of time, everything going on everywhere, and because of the miracles of communication it is possible for me to know, sitting here thousands of miles away. Not a spectacle, but an abiding interest. How can you not be involved? These are your times, your world, even if those events are on the other side of it. And as for the narrative—you are a part of that, for better or for worse, whether the gray inexorable economic inevitabilities—recessions and recoveries and having less money or more—or the grand perilous global story.

That story was at its most perilous—or so it seemed—by the time I was a sentient adult. The Soviet invasion of Hungary exactly coincided with the Suez crisis. A deliberate coincidence, perhaps, and certainly one that meant the eyes of the world were focused elsewhere. But a reminder that the central matter of the day was the Cold War.

From the first test explosion of a Soviet atom bomb in 1949 to the Test Ban Treaties of the 1960s and the 1972 Anti-Ballistic Missile Treaty many people lived in a state of nuclear angst. I did. Not initially, not perhaps seriously until after the Korean War, not until there were constant reminders—the first thermonuclear tests, the stark assessments of what a hydrogen bomb could do, the crises, Khrushchev's threats, the constant lurking menace behind everything, over and beyond anything else. You got on with life—of course—you managed to put it all aside, and then it would come slamming back at you from the newspapers, from some new turn of events. It was always potentially there, that tight knot in the stomach.

I looked at my small children, on a beach in Swansea, and thought that there was a real chance they would never grow up. I have that moment still: the sand, the sea, them with their buckets and spades, and the sense of apocalypse. I have the moment, it is still there, but I can't now believe in it. Post-apocalypse—if that is where we are—it is hard to recover that abiding shadow, the specter that stalked the days. Again, I go to the books, to find out where it went, what really happened.

Put at its simplest, this happened: because in any war between the Soviets and the West nuclear weapons would have been used, no such war took place. The Cold War was precisely that—cold. Mutually Assured Destruction saved the day, which was what was being gambled at the time, but when you were living through the gamble, that was all that you were aware of—the rolling of the dice, the arms race, the ratcheting-up of manic firepower, the concept of retaliation, tit for tat, city for city, Armageddon.

Jack and I did not join CND, go on Aldermaston marches. I can remember being uncertain, undecided, and then persuaded by his doubts about unilateral disarmament. In those early days of the bomb, Russian bombers could not reach the United States; the United Kingdom, with its American bases, would be likely to be the primary target. Discussion raged, always, accentuating that knot of fear.

And then, in 1962, there came the nine days of the Cuba crisis. Jack went to the university each morning, and I would wonder if I would see him again. My neighbor drove our five-year-olds to the school a mile away; the plan was that she would dash to fetch them if the four-minute warning went, while I minded our younger ones. You read in the papers of those who had retreated to the Highlands, or the west of Ireland. At one o'clock, at six o'clock, I would switch on the TV— those pulsating concentric rings that heralded the news back then, I can see them still—and I would watch the footage of the Russian missile-bearing ships, the faces of Kennedy, of Khrushchev. Waiting. Waiting.

Khrushchev backed off. It was over. It hadn't happened, but by a whisker, or so it felt. And still does, to those who have analyzed that time, and those who were at the heart of events. And we know now, as we did not back then, of the elaborate preparations for a nuclear holocaust. The government—around four thousand people from various government departments—would have holed up in a bunker close to Box Hill near Corsham in Wiltshire, sixty miles of tunnels that had been used in the last war as an ammunition depot, a factory and an RAF operations center. Assuming that there had been sufficient warning, sufficient buildup to a nuclear exchange, for them to get there; assuming that people agreed to go, leaving any surviving families to the mercy of radiation and the anticipated breakdown of any kind of social order. Ten Soviet hydrogen bombs on Britain would have killed nearly a third of the population and left a swathe of others seriously injured. With the government festering beneath Box Hill, the police and the military would have assumed control. Not that control seems a feasible term; thinking about this scenario, you move at once into fiction, as plenty have done, since: the absence of all facilities, a free-for-all where food was concerned, marauding gangs, violence, the rule of law a distant nirvana. It has been imagined many times, in print and film, and chills the blood.

Peter Hennessy has written graphically of the Cuba week, of how, if Khrushchev had not changed course at lunchtime on October 28,

1962, Prime Minister Macmillan would have set World War III drills in motion—the Transition to War Committee was nearly called that weekend. But it wasn't, the world breathed again, and one reads now with astonishment, and a kind of nervous hilarity, Hennessy's description of the arrangement whereby, should the prime minister have been in his car, on the move, at a moment of crisis, he would have been reached by way of the Automobile Association's radio network, whereupon his driver would have sought a phone booth from which the prime minister could make the essential call: ". . . only the Brits . . . could have dreamed up a system whereby the Prime Minister is envisaged making a collect call from a phone booth to authorize nuclear retaliation."

Indeed, one reads of all these meticulous, bureaucratic preparations with a certain incredulity. They had to, of course, that is what civil servants are for, what a government has to do. But it is eerie now to think that all this was going on—the discussions, the paperwork—while the rest of us were listening to the Cold War rattling of sabers, understanding what thermonuclear meant, looking with fear at our children playing on a beach. The plan for removal of art treasures before nuclear attack—eleven vans with military escort to quarries in Wales and Wiltshire; the Corsham bunker with its bedsteads, its ovens, its cups and saucers, equipped for post-holocaust government.

Government? Who, or what, would they have governed?

Escalation: the word that haunted, all through the sixties, the seventies, until at last the Vietnam War came to an end. Would the Russians come in? Would there be a direct Soviet–United States confrontation, spiraling up from that distant, localized conflict? It was as though the Cold War was already starting to smolder, the embers poised for a conflagration if the wind blew the wrong way.

Again, it didn't happen. The history of the late twentieth century seems like a sequence of reprieves, until the one great, startling positive of the fall of the Berlin Wall, the collapse of communism. I remember Jack, a political theorist, watching the events of 1989 and the end of the Soviet Union with amazement, almost with disbelief. And with exhilaration. He was the author of what is still seen as a seminal work on the definition of democracy; he had an interest.

Thirty years earlier—the summer of 1959—there had been a summer school in Oxford for a party of Soviet academics and their students—quite a radical departure at that point, surprising that the Russians agreed to it. Jack was one of those giving lectures and leading seminars. I think that the general theme was Britain and its institutions, so he must surely have given them a rundown on democracy, but what I remember is his wry amusement at the appreciative reception of Harold Nicolson, a visiting lecturer whose subject was the monarchy, and the irritation of the Oxford organizers at the KGB man—ostensibly a professor of something or other—who sat through all sessions reading *Pravda* and smoking a cigarette. Jack did everything he could to make contact with the small group of students, who were under draconian supervision but occasionally managed to break free. I remember Vanya, a particularly charming and exuberant boy, vanishing into the garden with the hostess's Italian au pair girl at one evening party, and being hauled back by the KGB man. On the last night, at another party, everyone fairly tipsy, we hugged Vanya and said we hoped, we really hoped, we'd see him again. His exuberance fell away; he pulled a face—"No, no, you will never see me again." He was well aware of the system under which he was living, would continue to live.

In 1984 I had my own glimpse of that system, as a member of a delegation of six writers sent by the Great Britain–USSR Association (which was sponsored by the Foreign Office) to have talks with representatives of the Soviet Writers' Union. We were there for ten days, first in Moscow having conference-style talks (immense long table, everyone wired up to microphones and headphones for simultaneous translation) and interminable toast-punctuated evening banquets, and then a few days' rest and recreation at Yalta on the Crimean coast as guests of the Ukrainian Writers' Union.

My diary of that visit is in a separate exercise book; we had been warned that if we were keeping notes we should have them with us at all times—our rooms and our luggage would undoubtedly be searched. They were; I found the contents of my suitcase slightly rearranged. Reading those scrawled pages now, I am at once taken back to the baffling, frequently tense, always inscrutable practices of that encounter with Soviet life. I wrote of the initial speech by their spokesman: " 'We know a great deal about you all,' says Kuznetzov after his remarks of greeting. Which was somehow unsettling rather than flattering." And of Red Square: "an eerie place, that rippling scarlet flag in the black night, hushed religious atmosphere in the small group in front of Lenin's tomb, people standing in silence or speaking in quiet voices. Statuesque policemen facing each other at the entrance, which was a crack open—a suspended feeling as though someone might come out—Lenin? The mausoleum is a monolithic slab-like structure. It—and the posture of the policeman—made me think of Pharaonic tombs in Upper Egypt."

We were shepherded throughout by two minders—a middle-aged woman called Tatiana, who was a translator, we were told, and Georgy, head of one of the state publishing houses, specializing in English translation, and both of them, we had been warned back in London, members of the KGB. My experience of Georgy veered from bizarre to chilling, when he accompanied us to the Crimea: "Somewhat odd to hurtle through the Crimea [in the coach from the airport] with Georgy, emitting the vodka fumes of his last three heavy evenings, bellowing an exegesis of the early works of Evelyn Waugh into my ear (apparently he is very popular here). It is really hard to credit that a Siberian public library he recently visited had copies of *Vile Bodies* and *Black Mischief* so heavily read as to be physical wrecks, but so he said." On another occasion, though, walking with him along the Yalta seafront, from which one gazed out over the Black Sea toward an empty horizon, somewhere beyond which, way beyond, lay Turkey, I commented (deliberately, provocatively) on the total absence of sailing boats or power boats off this coast, that would be a usual feature of resort shores: " 'No, here there are not. People are just not interested, you see, Penelope, it is a thing they do not much like to do.' Shrugging."

Some of the Soviet delegates did their best to drag politics into the agenda: "an address on the function of the critic was for the most part a diatribe about the arms race, the evil forces of violence and a denunciation of capitalist greed and irresponsibility." We were aware that all of them were necessarily figures acceptable to the regime, and some of them out-and-out apparatchiks: "People keep vanishing and being replaced by others in the Russian delegation. On the first day a woman scientist was there who appeared to have been drafted in at the last moment to refute our provocative item on the agenda about the paucity of Russian women writers [initially there had been no woman member of their team; we were fielding three]. She appeared from her remarks to be a biochemist but said she also wrote novels and claimed this was a mass phenomenon—'the unity of the artists and the scientists.'"

They all disregarded the agreement that none of us, on either side, would speak on any topic for more than four minutes—this, we soon realized, was simply not compatible with Russian style: "I have learned never to take at face value the expression 'a short comment upon the last speaker's remarks.'" Simultaneous translation meant that relays of translators staggered exhausted from their booths, and produced some interesting renderings: "We cannot throw away a baby with the water from the basin." And each evening there were those formal dinners: eat, a Russian rises to make a toast, a Brit rises to respond, eat a bit more, repeat the ritual. London had told us sternly that, while it would be all right for the women to take a token sip of each vodka toast, offense would be taken if the men did not down the glass—they must drink for England. Much mineral water was consumed by the British delegation during the morning sessions.

We arrived at the final session to find that everything was set for it to be televised: "As soon as the cameras were rolling Kuznetzov launched into an account of how our discussions had been of literature and writing but we had of course concerned ourselves with matters of the writer's commitment to society and especially the over-whelming question of international peace and how to counter the forces of aggression. Consecutive translation, so we had to wait a few minutes to get it, and then all froze with annoyance. Francis King splendidly countered with a sharp piece about how he couldn't recall that we had discussed any such thing, and we each said something to the same effect (which no doubt they will edit out of the program)."

In the Crimea we stayed at one of the thousand-bedroom hotels built for the recreation of the Soviet masses, sat about on a "skimpy pebbly beach littered with very fat Germans and Russians. Lukewarm completely inactive sea full of small jellyfish in which you loll wondering what to do next. Sat and listened to Georgy (wearing jockey shorts and a scarlet peaked cap) holding forth on his degree dissertation at Moscow University and the relative merits of Muriel Spark and Doris Lessing." And it was in the Crimea that there was the curious episode of the man who fell into conversation with some of us as we walked on the promenade one evening. Speaking good English, he explained that he was a seaman who had worked on a Russian refrigerated container ship plying the Baltic that had stopped off frequently at Hull, where he had English friends. Next day we were taken by coach to a palace along the coast, a place amidst an immense park with a cliff path along which we walked to admire the view: "And half-way along out from behind a tree appeared, incredibly, the seaman from the refrigerated container ship, clad only in diminutive shorts and dripping with sweat, whom we had met on the promenade in Yalta the night before. We could scarcely believe our eyes. The sense of paranoia and disorientation induced by this country is now complete. Anyway, he ambled along beside us, a very nice fellow, talking of his affection for the English and taste for English books, etc. with Tatiana, distinctly rattled, muttering, 'I think this is a very boring man, we must get free from him.'"

Coincidence? Or not? Had he wanted something of us? We speculated. We never knew.

Years later, I turned that episode into a short story, one that was to do with quite other things but was prompted by that time and place, an instance of the way in which, for me, short stories have always risen from some real-life moment but have then expanded into something quite detached from that.

And this was the abiding sense of opacity and ambiguity that made that taste of Soviet life so unnerving. You never really knew if things were as you thought they were, or quite other. Some people were genuinely open and friendly; others were opaque. The ten days were demanding, exhausting, intriguing; and occasionally hilarious. One evening, after a reception at the British Embassy, we managed to elude our minders and ended up in a restaurant where a large party of Romanians at a neighboring table were singing national songs: "Melvyn [Bragg] insisted we must counter so we belted out John Brown's Body, Tipperary, etc. until the Romanians announced themselves defeated and departed with much flashing of teeth and hand-shaking."

My Soviet diary ends: "Things I never want to see again: a Russian bath towel, which is two feet by one foot and made of sandpaper; the lift at the Yalta hotel, full of large sweating people all pushing each other; the beach at Yalta; Georgy; the grey carcasses of cooked chicken offered for breakfast in the hotel canteen; a microphone; Georgy."

A diary is an ambivalent reflection of memory.

Much that is in mine I no longer remember; the diary is testimony but memory has wiped. And, conversely, stuff lies still in the head that apparently escaped the diary. From the Soviet visit, I have further shreds: our final hours before the plane home, when we spent our remaining roubles (a daily subsistence "fee" which could not be changed into hard currency) on large bowls of caviar for afternoon tea; Tatiana, on the plane to the Crimea, ordering several rows of fellow passengers to their feet with a mere gesture and tilt of her head, in order to have us seated together rather than scattered around the plane and thus not under her eye—how did they know that she was a person you had to obey? And I remember a visit to Chekhov's house in the Crimea—a rare privilege, apparently, not generally open—small cluttered rooms with photos and personal possessions and I wanted to keep quiet, and had that sudden blinding recognition that the past is true, that Chekhov had indeed existed, had been here, once, where we now were.

I have never been back to Russia; the Soviet Union that we fleetingly experienced is now a historical phenomenon. Someone of my age, living there now, will have known an extraordinary social and political upheaval, in an incredibly short space of time. Born into one world, they live now in another—from totalitarianism to democracy, of a kind. Accelerated change, unlike the slow social metamorphosis of this country—indeed, of most politically stable countries in peacetime.

But change there has been, here, and when I squint back at my twenty-year-old self I realize that she would be surprised by two of the major ways in which assumptions and expectations have mutated, and would be startled, probably, to understand that she herself would shortly be a manifestation of a third. I want now to look at this: the three ways in which, to my mind, our society has revised itself during my lifetime—one seismic, one determined and by and large successful, one opaque and generating argument.

Opacity and argument first. The shifting ground of class and social distinctions. Is the twenty-first century any closer to achieving the classless society to which John Major looked forward in 1990? On the face of it—no. That said, the social landscape of the 1950s looks very different from that of today—more predictable, more rigid, you could place a person by how they spoke, how they dressed. There is a flexibility today that is less to do with social mobility than with a more open-minded approach; perhaps we are just less bothered by apparent distinctions. But the polarizations are still there—the violent apposition of those who have and those who have not.

Any comments I make on social change come from a single perspective. Not unusual—most people live out their lives within a particular context of society. Social mobility? Well, yes—there are plenty also who have changed ground, hopped up a rung or three—social mobility is usually talking about improved rather than reduced circumstances. I have a friend my own age who says, "People like you and me have gone down in the world." What he means is that we live a lot more humbly than our grandparents did, though his were rather more amply situated than mine. But that is to do with a general historical trend rather than families in decline. The middle class does not live like it did in the early twentieth century: the servicing, the expectations. Well, some do, I suppose, but none that I know. And there's the difference. The middle class in which, and with which, I have lived is not the same as the one my grandmother knew.

So I have lived on ground that was shifting, but it did so rather suddenly, in the midcentury, before I was firmly enough established to notice. I never expected to live like my grandparents had. Just as well. We began married life on Jack's salary as a university lecturer, and academic salaries have never been other than frugal. But we could manage the mortgage on an Edwardian semi in Swansea with a little garden; that is middle-class living, then or now. And he was in what would be regarded as a profession, if that is a defining feature of the middle class, even if he had arrived there from quite elsewhere.

What I am trying to say is that I have observed rather than experienced. My only swerve was to marry a young man from the northern working class, the two of us meeting up in the fresh air of the midcentury, both liberated into the social neutrality of higher education. But he had, and continued to have, the advantage of a dual perspective; if he were here still he would be looking over my shoulder at this point and making stringent comments.

However, to observe is to experience, in one sense. If those around you are behaving differently, if assumptions and expectations and opinions mutate then you are going to mutate with them, unless you are peculiarly intransigent or holed up in some fortress of religious or political belief. I have been formed in and by late twentieth-century Britain; I reflect my times. I can't think or see as my grandmother did. She was born when Disraeli was prime minister, died in the age of Harold Wilson. For her, class differences were not only inevitable but desirable; she seemed to be unaware of homosexuality and I never knew if this was genuine ignorance or tacit rejection; her view of gender distinction was that men were a different breed from women, you deferred to them in some respects and recognized that they had special needs—cooked breakfast and somewhere to go and smoke. Sex was unmentionable. And alongside all this ran an ingrained sense of obligation; you were more comfortable than most, it was therefore beholden upon you to help others. She did. A Christian ethic—and she was of course paid-up Church of England—and also a manifestation of the arbitrary system of gift aid inherited from the nineteenth century that the welfare state was to supplant.

I imagine that my own grandchildren when elderly will cast a critical eye upon my own mind-set of today. How I would love to know in what ways it appears—will appear—archaic or perverse. Ours is on the whole a pretty tolerant and liberal-minded age; can tolerance be stretched yet further? Some would say, indeed yes. That there are still areas of ignorance and insensitivity. Or could there be a reversion—could we come to seem unprincipled, licentious, devoid of standards? Somewhere, at some level, the seeds of change will be starting already to sprout. Society does not support stasis.

My grandmother's house, and the sense in which its contents seemed to have become signifiers for the century, inspired a book for me—*A House Unlocked*—and I discussed there the shifting pattern of social expectations over her lifetime, and the way in which my perception of the world differed from hers. My own marriage had come to seem to me nicely symbolic of the reforms of the midcentury, which meant that two people who could not otherwise have met came together because of the Butler Education Act of 1946.

There is plenty of informed argument about the degree of social change in the last fifty years: the answers can be opaque, conflicting. But there are two areas of change that seem to me in one case indisputable and in the other seismic: the expectations of women, and attitudes toward homosexuality.

When I was a small girl, there was a teatime ritual. She—it was always a she—who took the last cake, bun, sandwich from the plate was entitled to a wish; you had a choice of wish—a handsome husband or ten thousand a year. Nobody ever chose the ten thousand. There were various related strictures, too: if you don't sit straight you'll grow up round-shouldered and no one will ever marry you; if you make faces the wind will change and you'll get stuck like that and no one will ever marry you. The central female concern was being made clear.

An atavistic concern. Marriage—partnership—is a natural and normal aspiration. Most people would prefer to go through life in alliance with someone they love, and most want children. But the teatime wish husband was about status, not inclinations. Unmarried, you would have reduced social status—the ancient social stigma, the heart of the matter in any Jane Austen novel. And, of course, in the past the spinster's position was precarious economically. But cash flow can't have much entered into the teatime wish choice, or more would have plumped for the ten thousand. Indeed, my recollection is that it was seen as ludicrous to do so, if not a touch disgraceful.

A recent television program featured an organization that makes a packet out of running seminars for people who want to become rich enough fast enough to be able to live off their cash without ever working. The accumulation of a property portfolio was the scheme, and it was clear that most of those paying a wad in order to learn how to go about this were already in catastrophic financial debt to the organization. Many were young women, and their attitudes startled me. Not only did they feel they "ought" to be millionaires, but they felt that they ought not to have to work; work was not their aspiration, what they wanted was a certain lifestyle, a nicely well-heeled lifestyle free of obligation.

Dupes, I fear, poor dears, and I hope there weren't too many of them. But they did make me think about feminism, and what it originally meant, and to wonder what those girls would have thought about that. Feminist aspiration, back in the sixties and seventies, was all about work: equal opportunity in the workplace, equal pay, equality of esteem across the board. The feminist did not want to be a trophy wife, or a millionaire; she wanted respect and recognition for who she was, and what she could do.

Have we got what they were demanding? Today, it seems that two-thirds of low-paid workers are women, and that women in full-time work earn sixteen percent less than men. So the answer would seem to be no, not entirely. And one hears constantly of women bringing claims against employers on the grounds that male colleagues were preferred for promotion, and for unfair dismissal when pregnant. The glass ceiling exists, apparently, and every woman has to balance career against motherhood.

But I am concerned with assumptions and perceptions, and it is impossible to deny that a young woman today steps out into a very different society from that of fifty years ago. Depending, of course, on what sort of young woman she is. The feminist movement was ever a middle-class movement, and there is a big divide today between the professional woman, who may well be earning the same as a man, and the vastly larger female workforce that is cleaning offices, stacking shelves and sitting at checkouts and mostly does not. Plenty of ground still to be gained, but the seminal matter is that a point has been made, slowly and inexorably, over the last decades: it is no longer possible to treat women differently from men and not be held to account.

There's more, much more. Women have surged into higher education. At my university, in the 1950s, we were one woman to ten men. This did give us a certain commodity value—ten chaps to pick from—but what I wonder now is why we didn't question this. Why didn't we look at that morass of males and think: they can't all be so much brighter than lots of girls who aren't here. Today, that university has near parity between men and women, actually tipped slightly in favor of women.

We were the pre-feminist generation. Long post-suffragette, but apparently not awake to the still-prevailing anachronisms. There were exceptions, of course, those already sniffing the air, but on the whole my generation now seems to me to have been somewhat inert. Ten years later the climate would be very different.

One thing above all, though, reminded us that it was hazardous to be a woman. We girls of the midcentury lived with one eye on the calendar. There was far less discussion of sex back then but it was quite as brisk a component of student life as it is today. We just made less fuss about it, kept it under cover, mindful of what was likely to happen to any girl who got pregnant. She would probably be sent down, dismissed from the university, quietly and conclusively. And the man? Oh, no. Those were pre-pill days; contraception was unreliable, and most of us were pretty uninformed about it. So girls brave enough to embark on a relationship lurched from month to month, eyeing the calendar and hoping for the best. And this was going on up and down the land, of course. No difficulties back then for childless couples hoping to adopt; the relevant institutions were well stocked with babies discreetly unloaded.

Sometime in the early sixties Jack, who taught PPE—politics, philosophy, and economics—was interviewing a candidate for a place at his Oxford college, a bluntly spoken northern lad. He asked the boy which aspect of contemporary society he saw as most in need of reform. The answer bounced back without a moment's hesitation: "Reform of the abortion laws and legalization of homosexuality." The boy got a place, needless to say.

We all knew that you could get an abortion. We had all heard of someone who had. We knew that it involved furtive inquiries, a clandestine visit to a closely guarded address, the handing over of an envelope of bank notes—a couple of hundred quid, a fortune in those days, if the address was not in some back street but somewhere you stood a better chance of a medically qualified practitioner and, indeed, of survival. We all knew the myths about self-induced abortion: the glass of gin and a hot bath, the trampolining on the bed. And that they did not work, by and large. The shadow of that fate hung over any burgeoning love affair—just, frankly, as it always had done. We were in exactly the same position as the Victorian domestic servant, or the medieval village girl.

So what a catalyst for change—the pill. And how quickly we have forgotten just what a revolution it heralded. Not just in giving women the power of choice, but in reshaping attitudes toward sex and sexuality. For the first time in human history a young woman—any woman— can enter into a sexual relationship without fretting constantly that she will be landed with an untimely baby. And it is openly acknowledged that sexual activity takes place, everywhere and all the time, which may sound an absurd statement, but set it against the paranoid reticence of much of early twentieth-century society, when someone like my grandmother—far from untypical—went through life avoiding all mention or recognition of that most basic human concern. And she had three children.

She and her like represented, I suppose, the last gasp of Victorian middle-class sublimation, soldiering on into the twentieth century and surrounded by an insidious tide of provocative new behavior. Elsewhere, things were already different. Take that emblematic Bloomsbury drawing-room gathering when Lytton Strachey pointed a finger at a stain on Vanessa Bell's dress and announced: "Semen?" Sometime in the 1920s. In most drawing rooms the word would have been unfamiliar to many and unmentionable for all. Bloomsbury was ahead of the game, and even today Strachey might seem a touch candid. But the point is that the shift had already begun, the unstoppable slide toward entire permissiveness, to a climate in which nothing is unmentionable and most of it is mentioned all the time. And this has happened over sixty years or so—not unlike the reverse journey from the cheerful profanity of the eighteenth century to the constraint of the Victorian age. Maybe it will switch once more and my descendants will find themselves with pursed lips and averted eyes.

Feminism; the pill; sexual candor. But there is one aspect of change in assumptions and attitudes over my lifetime that seems to me seismic—so rapid, so absolute.

When I was nine, one summer in Alexandria, I fell in love with a young man. He was twenty-eight, and a sort of relative—his sister was married to my uncle, Oliver Low. Hugh Gibb was serving with the Eighth Army in the Libyan campaign, and on his leaves from the desert, he would visit us, often joining my mother at Sidi Bishr, Alexandria's prime beach, where she held lunch parties from a rented cabin. Hugh was popular, charming, and I was besotted. We surfed together; I was pretty good with a surfboard, and those moments are with me still—the careful choice of wave, and then the glorious slide down its flank, with Hugh a few feet away, head turned sideways, beaming encouragement as the wave broke and we rushed toward the shore.

A few years later, in London now, Hugh turned up for a family lunch at my grandmother's house in Harley Street. Uncle Oliver was there—various others. And Hugh—still charming, still everyone's favorite person, still being nice to me (who was by then perhaps fourteen). After he had gone, I remarked to Oliver, complacently, that Hugh was not married (could he be waiting till I was old enough . . .).

Oliver laughed: "My dear girl, Hugh's queer."

Queer? *Queer?* In what way?

Did I ask for an explanation? Was one given? I don't know—and actually Oliver was being quite risqué, talking like that to a fourteen-year-old, but he was the bohemian end of my father's family, my favorite uncle, and he liked me, as a seemingly bookish sort of girl with whom he enjoyed a chat. Suffice it that, somehow, I knew from then on that there were men who weren't interested in women, and if Hugh was one of them then that was that. I fell out of love at once, sensibly enough, though I continued to like Hugh and to bask if he noticed me.

When my granddaughter Izzy was not much older than I had been then, I took her to a production of *The Importance of Being Earnest*. She knew little of Oscar Wilde, so on the way to the theatre I filled in with some facts—the life, the scandal, the trial, the imprisonment. When I was done she exploded: "I don't believe you! He was sent to prison because he was *gay!*"

A fifty-year gap, or thereabouts. One adolescent who had never heard of homosexuality; another who didn't realize that it had once been illegal. A chasm of understanding and assumption.

So by the time I was grown-up I was well aware of homosexuality. There was the occasional scandal—some high-profile figure arrested, some peer or actor whose misfortune was relished and prolonged by the newspapers. But it seems to me that my student generation was still wonderfully naïve. Looking back, I can identify contemporaries both male and female who were undoubtedly gay, but this was never spoken of, or at least not in the circles in which I moved, and in some cases I wonder if they themselves recognized their own nature. And this was the early 1950s; legalization "between consenting adults" was only just over ten years off.

Within half a century the most abiding sexual taboo has vanished. Yes, there are still pockets of homophobia, but by and large same-sex relationships are accepted as a norm. The 2011 census asked if you were in a same-sex civil partnership or, indeed, a registered same-sex civil partnership (along with your ethnic group, if mixed/multiple: White and Black Caribbean, White and Black African, White and Asian . . . one imagined households up and down the land puzzling over their correct definition). The census is the status quo made manifest, or rather, the bureaucratic drive to identify the status quo. In 1951 they were exercised about the fertility and duration of marriage, the dates of cessation of full-time education, and how many outside loos the nation still had; a question compiler of back then, fast-forwarded to 2011 and confronted with registered same-sex civil partnerships, would have gasped in disbelief.

But the census tells it as it is, an unblinking social snapshot, and this is the way we live now, by grace of the extraordinary tidal wave of change unleashed by the legislation of 1967. Change not just in what people may do now, but in how others view them, which seems to me the most remarkable aspect—the overturning of an entire history of prejudice and denial. An upheaval neatly slotted into my lifetime, so that I grew up to the backdrop of one set of assumptions and sign off in a very different society.

Memory

A couple of years ago, Izzy yearned for an old-fashioned manual typewriter: "Vintage!" A Smith Corona was found off eBay, and she rejoiced in it until a new ribbon became necessary, and then no one could work out how to change the ribbon. I was summoned: "I can't believe we're going to Granny for technical support." I sat at the machine, looked, did not know how it was done, but lo! my fingers did. They remembered. You lifted out the old reel, put the new one on, thus, you slotted the ribbon through there, and there, pushed that lever, wound the end of the ribbon round the empty reel and caught it on that prong. There! My brain hadn't remembered, but my fingers had—veterans of manual typewriters. That was how it felt, anyway.

This is an instance of what is called procedural memory, that aspect of memory whereby we remember how to do something. How to ride a bicycle is the example frequently cited, but I prefer my typewriter experience, or Vladimir Nabokov's of pushing a pram, he being that most refined authority on memory: "You know, I still feel in my wrists certain echoes of the pram-pusher's knack, such as, for example, the glib downward pressure one applied to the handle in order to have the carriage tip up and climb the curb." Yes, yes—and a sensation alien to those who have known only the abrupt tilt required for the strollers of today. My first pram, as a very young mother, was one of those sleek majestic cruisers, and my wrists too respond.

There is procedural memory, and then there is semantic memory, which enables us to know that this thing with two wheels is a bike, and that object is a typewriter—the memory facility that retains facts, language, all forms of knowledge without reference to context. And finally, and crucially, there is episodic or autobiographical memory, which gives the context, reminds me that my student bike was dark blue with my initials painted in white, that the baby in the sleek pram once grabbed the shopping, and squeezed ripe tomatoes all over everything. Autobiographical memory is random, nonsequential, capricious, and without it we are undone.

Much of what goes on in the mind is recollection, memory. This is not thought—it is an involuntary procession of images, ranging from yesterday to long ago, interspersed with more immediate signals like: must remember to phone so-and-so, or, what shall I have for lunch? Pure thought is something else—it requires conscious effort and is hard to achieve. The Borges story about the boy cursed—not blessed, cursed—

with total recall, with a memory of everything, demonstrates how punishing that would be, how he remembers "not only every leaf of every tree in every patch of forest, but every time he had perceived or imagined that leaf." And, crucially, he did not think: "To think is to ignore (or forget) differences, to generalize, to abstract." It is the mind's holy grail, thought, and the process hardest to control—erratic, and prone to every kind of hijack. What bubbles up most of the time is memory, no more and no less.

Memory and anticipation. What has happened, and what might happen. The mind needs its tether in time, it must know where it is—in the perpetual slide of the present, with the ballast of what has been and the hazard of what is to come. Without that, you are adrift in the wretched state of Alzheimer's, or you are an amnesiac.

Amnesia disrupts autobiographical memory. In retrograde amnesia, everything is forgotten that happened before amnesia struck; in anterograde amnesia, memories can no longer be stored, the past is kept, but the future—passing time—cannot become a part of it. In dementia, life takes place in a segment of time without past or future. For mental stability we need the three kinds of memory to be fighting fit—procedural, semantic, autobiographical. And never mind that auto-biographical memory is full of holes—it is meant to be like that. There is what we remember, and there is the great dark cavern of what we have forgotten, and why some stuff goes there and something else does not is the territory of the analysts, where I cannot venture. We forget—we forget majestically—and that seems to be an essential part of memory's function, whether it is the significant forgetting of sublimation, or denial, or whatever, or the mundane daily forgetting of where the car keys have got to, or those elusive names that so challenge us. William James is elegant on that particular problem: "Suppose we try to recall a forgotten name. The state of our consciousness is peculiar. There is a gap there, but no mere gap. It is a gap that is intensely active. A sort of a wraith of a name is in it, beckoning in a given direction." I love the concept of the active gap, the wraith, and know them well: that evasive name of mine has a T somewhere about it, or possibly a P . . . And it is good to feel companionate with a brilliant thinker of a hundred years ago, irritably flogging his mind because he can't remember what that man he met last week is called. But he doesn't put forward any theory as to why it is names that are most vulnerable. I am still waiting.

The memory that we live with—the form of memory that most interests me—is the moth-eaten version of our own past that each of us carries around, depends on. It is our ID; this is how we know who we are and where we have been.

That, presumably, is why we spend so much time foraging around in it, in that unconsidered, involuntary way—we are checking it out, touching base, letting it demonstrate that it is still in good working order. This morning, while going about ordinary morning business—shower, eat breakfast, read newspaper—I have visited Seattle, where once years ago I was taken to the fish market, this memory prompted by an item on the radio about fish stocks—I saw those huge Alaskan salmon again, laid out on the slab; I have seen my aunt Rachel, and heard her voice, conjured up by a painting of hers that I pass on the way down to the kitchen; the orange in the fruit bowl there became the one through which I once stuck a skewer, trying to reproduce for four-year-old granddaughter Rachel the turning of the world, she having asked—inconveniently, while I was making the gravy for the Christmas turkey—why it gets dark at night. None of this is sought, hunted down—it just pops up, arbitrary, part of the stock-pile. And each memory brings some tangential thought, or at least until that is clipped short by the ongoing morning and its demands. The whole network lurks, all the time, waiting for a thread to be picked up, followed, allowed to vibrate. My story; your story.

Except that it is an entirely unsatisfactory story. The novelist in me—the reader, too—wants shape and structure, development, a theme, insights. Instead of which there is this assortment of slides, some of them welcome, others not at all, defying chronology, refusing structure. The Seattle salmon, my aunt, that Christmas orange are simply shuffled together—make what you like of it.

We do just that, endlessly—it is the abiding challenge and mystery, memory. I have to invoke Sir Thomas Browne again: "Darkness and light divide the course of time, and oblivion shares with memory, a great part even of our living beings; we slightly remember our felicities, and the smartest stroaks of affliction leave but short smart upon us . . . To be ignorant of evils to come, and forgetful of evils past, is merciful provision in nature, whereby we digest the mixture of our few and evil days, and, our delivered senses not relapsing into cutting remembrances, our sorrows are not kept raw by the edge of repetitions." Exquisitely put, but I'd take issue with some of that, which seems to be letting memory off rather lightly—the cutting remembrances are around all right, I'd say, and the stroaks of affliction. It is the view of memory as we'd like it to be, rather than as it is. Or is there a premature glimmer of psychological theories far in the future—ideas about suppressed memories? "Forgetful of evils past . . ."—denial? Suffice it that he is thinking about the operation of memory, and with such style that you can't but mull over the words, the phrases.

Joseph Brodsky thought memory "a substitute for the tail that we lost for good in the happy process of evolution. It directs our movements, including migration. Apart from that, there is something clearly atavistic in the very process of recollection, if only because such a process is never linear." His own migration from youth as an active opponent of the regime in Soviet Russia, with accompanying punishments, to exile in America as a celebrated poet and commentator, gave him a striking memory trail, though he says, oddly, "I remember rather little of my own life and what I do remember is of small consequence." But he had considered memory: "What memory has in common with art is the knack for selection, the taste for detail . . . Memory contains precisely details, not the whole picture; highlights, if you will, not the entire show."

All the best commentary on the working of memory seems to me to share this emphasis on "the knack for selection, the taste for detail." Nabokov's "series of spaced flashes"—and I want to get on to them later. Just as the most effective method of memoir writing seems to be to focus on that, to try to reflect the processes of memory itself rather than the artificial plod through time of routine autobiography. When I did that myself, nearly twenty years ago, in a memoir of childhood, it was because I realized that that childhood was there in my mind still, but in the form of these finite glimpses of that time, not sequential but coexisting, each of them succinct, clear, usually wordless, and conjuring up still those frozen moments of a time and a place. Most people remember childhood in that way, I think, and in old age these assorted shards in the head seem to become sharper still; they assert themselves when a conversation you had last week has been wiped, along with a friend's name and the whereabouts of your transit pass. Childhood memories have a high visual content—I certainly found that, as Egypt surged up in bits and pieces—the buff and brown bark of a eucalyptus tree, the brilliant green of a praying mantis, the white of roosting egrets on a tree by the Cairo Nile. Coleridge noted this feature, thinking about the nature of memory, and wondered if the visual quality was enhanced because of the lack of a spoken element: "I hold that association depends in a much greater degree on the recurrence of resembling *states of feeling* than in trains of ideas; that the recollection of early childhood in latest old age depends on and is explicable by this." And also, surely, because of the novelty, the fresh vision of the physical world—Wordsworth's "Splendour in the Grass"— when things are seen for the first time, the imprint that remains.

This would seem to account also for the capricious nature of time. It accelerates, it has broken into a gallop by the time you are old—a day then has nothing of the remembered pace of childhood days, which inched ahead, stood still at points, ambled from lunchtime to teatime. And laid down, every now and then, one of those indestructible moments of seeing. William James described this effect: "In youth we may have an absolutely new experience, subjective or objective, every hour of the day. Apprehension is vivid, the retentiveness strong, and our recollections of that time, like those of a time spent in rapid and interesting travel, are of something intricate, multitudinous and long-drawn out. But as each passing year converts some of this experience into automatic routine which we hardly note at all, the days and the weeks smooth themselves out in recollection to contentless units, and the years grow hollow and collapse."

The collapsing years of old age are indeed a source of dismay. They disconcert. What has happened to time, that it whisks away like this? And such answers as the psychologists have come up with seem to home in on the idea that the experience of time is linked to what is going on in our consciousness. Intensity of experience is a factor: traumatic events appear to be more recent than they in fact are. Intense expectation can make time pass more slowly; I can still remember the agonizing crawl of a week when I was waiting to go to Oxford station to meet a young man I was in love with—four more days . . . three . . . days that were each a week long. Nearly sixty years ago.

When you are busy, time scampers—a truism, but one that we all recognize. "A week is a long time in politics"—a cliché, but one that nicely suggests the flexible quality of time, its ability to expand, as it were, on demand. A political week can stretch to accommodate gathering events: more and more can happen, in obligingly baggy days, until on Sunday the prime minister resigns.

That is expansion of time. The old-age experience is the opposite—the sense of having entered some new dimension in which the cantering days and weeks are quite out of control. In some ways this puzzles me. Intensity of experience is not lost—there are still the bad times and the points of great pleasure, but they seem to have lost their capacity to arrest time, to make it pause, hover. On the other hand, memory has acquired some merciful ability to close up, to diminish the worst passages of more recent life. For me, the awful summer and autumn of Jack's illness—the hospital months, the last weeks at home—are now not time but a series of images I cannot lose. My own three and a half months of pain, four years ago, are also not months at all, but just the memory of a state of being, of how it was.

In childhood, a year is a large proportion of your life. Not so when you are eighty. That must have a lot to do with it. We old are cavalier about years; they have lost the capacity to impress. When you are eight, to be nine is a distant and almost unimaginable summit; Christmas is always far away, it will never come. For the old, it is a question of time's dismaying acceleration; we would prefer it to slow down now, to give us a chance to savor this glorious spring—we may not see so many more—while anticipation is now welcome and there's no rush for that next birthday, thank you. And maybe it is precisely because we find ourselves on this unstoppable conveyor belt that we are so much concerned with recollection, with reviewing all those memory shards in the head, brushing up time past, checking it out.

Much of my own childhood was spent in a garden, and I find that—miraculously, it seems—I can, today, seventy plus years later, draw a precise map of that garden, more or less to scale. Not only can I see it—the eucalyptus and casuarina trees, the rose arbor round the basin with the statue of Mercury, the water garden with the arum lilies and bamboo—but I know exactly how it was laid out. This was a very English garden, created by my mother, but in Egypt, a few miles outside Cairo. And I spent so much time in it because I was a solitary only child, and did not go to school. But what surprises me now is not that I have all these images of it in my head, but that I have also a map of it, which I can reproduce on paper (I know—I've done it). I can make a plan of this large garden—the drive leading up to the house, flanked by the lawn and the pond with the weeping willow, the rose garden, the kitchen garden, my secret hiding place in the hedge, the wild bit at the end where there are persimmon bushes that the mongooses raid—no uncertainties, no section uncharted.

Spatial memories are stored in that area of the brain called the hippocampus, specifically the right hippocampus. My eight/nine/ten-year-old hippocampus was at work back then, it would seem. Today, I often watch a couple of young men on motorbikes, consulting clipboards, outside my window. They are trainee taxi drivers, who have teamed up to do the Knowledge together, the repertoire of three hundred and twenty main routes within a six-mile radius of Charing Cross, covering twenty-five thousand streets, on which they will be examined before receiving their licence as a black-cab driver. The square on which I live is the end point of the first "run" in the Knowledge. A study done in 2000 at University College London of sixteen black-cab drivers who had spent two years doing the Knowledge, showed that all had a larger right hippocampus than control subjects, and the longer they had been on the job, the larger the hippocampus. I find this fascinating—the thought that the intricate maps of the city crammed into these heads could actually alter the brain. And I am amazed that my own young brain could operate in the same way, storing spatial memory that I still have.

The hippocampus for spatial memory. Is there some site in the brain dedicated to language, to sign systems? It can certainly feel as though there is, some memory cabinet in which certain knowledge is stashed away, seldom or never used, its contents not in good shape, but somehow easily available. When I went back to Egypt for the first time, as an adult, I found that words and phrases of Arabic came swimming up, that I must once have known and had not forgotten but had put away somewhere, ignored for decades. Equally, I never speak French now, but because once, when I was young, I spent a long time in France and emerged with good French, I still have the language, after a fashion; I wouldn't be able to speak it as I once did, but the ghost of it is there in my head—I know how you say this, say that. Unused equipment, but not defunct. And because I learned Latin at school, I can make a bit of sense of a Latin text, not absolute sense, but some understanding comes smoking up—a word I know, and that is a noun, and that a verb, and also I can recognize all those connections to the language that I speak, the ancestral sounds and meanings. I wish I had some shreds of Anglo-Saxon as well.

More oddly, I have this system of shapes, too— Pitman's shorthand, if you please. I could write this sentence in shorthand—ponderously and pointlessly. I learned typing and shorthand for a few months well over fifty years ago; typing proficiency has been invaluable, my shorthand never got anywhere near the point where anyone would have employed me to use it, but there it still lies, in my head, indestructible and rather irritating.

When did I first become interested in the operation of memory? Slowly, I think, gradually—noticing its various manifestations. My daughter, aged three, referred to a place we had been to "a long time ago not as long as all that." The visit had been about a month before; I liked her first attempt to marshal time, to put it in context, to pin memory to time. Children under five remember all right, there seems to be no question of that, but at some later point most or all of these memories disappear—childhood amnesia, this is called, a phenomenon that has fascinated psychologists since Freud's obsession with it. Nabokov saw his own "awakening of consciousness as a series of spaced flashes, with the intervals between them gradually diminishing until bright blocks of perception are formed, affording memory a slippery hold." The "flash" of his that I most relish is his memory of crawling through a tunnel behind a divan and emerging at the end "to be welcomed by a mesh of sunshine on the parquet under the cane work of a Viennese chair and two game-some flies settling by turn." Reading that, you realize that you are seeing through the eyes of a four-year-old in St. Petersburg before the Russian revolution.

The psychology of childhood memory is complex and strewn with different theories—why we remember this, forget that. Fear and shock seem to play a part—most of us remember something nasty to do with a dog, or one's gruesome injury to a knee. But many childhood memories are simple and visual—a frozen moment that has for some reason become hardwired into the mind, there forever. And this surely is related to the pristine experience of childhood, when everything is seen for the first time—those game-some St. Petersburg flies, Wordsworth's glory in the flower. Spring is still a marvel, when you are eighty, but it does not have the electric impact of novelty. What happens, it seems to me—my own diffident theory of memory development—is that the laying down of vivid visual experience in early childhood shifts to the accumulation of scenes from life as lived, the patchy collection of what has been seen and heard and felt that will add up to auto-biographical memory. Quite a bit still that is sharply visual, but with added soundtrack, and a freight of significance. The great stockpile on which we depend, perched upon that initial fragile structure of uncomplicated observation.

My own earliest childhood memories—those that have survived childhood amnesia—are either visual or tactile. I don't much remember what anyone said, or what I felt. Lucy, who looked after me, was admirable at creative play. There was little acquisition of toys or games; we *made* things. So I have the memory of what making papier-mâché feels like: the shredding of newspaper, the mixing of squeaky, tacky starch with water to make a paste in which you soak the shredded paper, the careful layering of the result into a relief map—we were particularly keen on maps—which could then be painted: brown hills, green valleys, blue rivers. We made Christmas wrapping paper with potato cuts: a halved potato cut into a star shape, or a holly leaf, a Christmas tree, then dipped in poster paint and stamped on a sheet of brown paper. Enjoyably messy—poster paint everywhere. For dolls' tea parties a thimble was used to cut tiny tarts out of orange peel, with a eucalyptus seed stuck in the center. The dolls themselves were made of card, drawn by Lucy, and then provided with a paper wardrobe made by me, extravagant creations that clipped on with tabs at shoulders and waist. Hours of intense application—the sleeve to go thus, the skirt like this, cut it out, and then reach for the paintbox and the final flourish of creativity. These memories of absorbed involvement are different from uncomplicated observation, but seem to me equally pristine, equally a part of the distant fragile structure of childhood in the mind.

There is individual memory and there is collective memory; our own locked cupboard and the open shelf available to all. What only I know, and what is known—or can be known—to anyone. This startling apposition between a myriad of memories, available only to the owner, and the immense record of the collective past, which is incomplete, argued over, but of which a vast amount is indisputable and familiar to millions. Only I know that once I spoke certain words, misguidedly, and am sorry now; everyone knows that men once landed on the moon. The huge collective hoard is impersonal; certain items may prompt dismay, distress, sympathy, but the emotions are detached—there is not the creep of intimacy, that I did this and should not have done, that this was done to me and it still hurts.

There is the further apposition that personal memory is the same extensive larder for each of us, unless we are given to denial, or otherwise affected in some way, but collective memory is unevenly distributed: some people have a rich and deep resource, for others it is minimal. A matter of education, and also of inclination. But however minimal, however threadbare, it is ballast of a kind. We all need that seven-eighths of the iceberg, the ballast of the past, a general past, the place from which we came.

That is why history should be taught in school, to all children, as much of it as possible. If you have no sense of the past, no access to the historical narrative, you are afloat, untethered; you cannot see yourself as a part of the narrative, you cannot place yourself within a context. You will not have an understanding of time, and a respect for memory and its subtle victory over the remorselessness of time.

I have been reading history all my life, and am sharply aware that I know very little. I have an exaggerated respect for historians—certain historians; they seem to me grounded in a way that most of us are not, possessed of an extra sense by virtue of access to times and places when things were done differently. They have—can have—heightened perception.

History is not so much memory as collective evidence. It is what has happened, what is thought to have happened, what some claim to have happened. The collective past is fact and fabrication—much like our private pasts. There is no received truth, just a tenuous thread of events amid a swirl of dispute and conflicting interpretation. But . . . the past is real. This is simplistic but also, for me, awe-inspiring. I am silenced when I think about it: the great ballast of human existence. Archaeology appeals to me precisely because it offers tacit but tangible evidence—the pots, the weapons, the bones, the stones. Jack, as a political theorist, needed the legacy of thought—he needed the minds of Aristotle, Rousseau, and Hobbes. I am fired more by the eloquence of objects—the pieces of seventeenth-century salt-glaze I used to dig up in our Oxfordshire garden that said: a person made this dish, people used this (and broke it), they were here, and that time actually happened.

To be completely ignorant of the collective past seems to me to be another state of amnesia; you would be untethered, adrift in time. Which is why all societies have sought some kind of memory bank, whether by way of folklore, story-telling, recitation of the ancestors—from Homer to Genesis. And why the heritage industry does so well today; most people may not be particularly interested in the narrative of the past, in the detail or the discussion, but they are glad to know that it is there.

For me, interest in the past segued into an interest in the operation of memory, which turned into subject matter for fiction. I wanted to write novels that would explore the ways in which memory works and what it can do to people, to see if it is the crutch on which we lean, or the albatross around the neck. It is both, of course, depending on circumstance, depending on the person concerned. In *The Photograph*, Glyn's memory of his dead young wife is distorted and perverted by the discovery of a challenging photograph. In *Moon Tiger*, Claudia's version of her past is questioned by the conflicting evidence of others. I have learned to be suspicious of memory—my own, anyone's—but to accord it considerable respect. Whether accurate or not, it can subvert a life. And for a novelist, the whole concept of memory is fascinating and fertile.

In a novel, the narrative moves from start to finish, from beginning to end. But within that framework time can be juggled, treated with careless disregard—the story can progress, can dip backward, fold up, expand. What matters is the satisfactory whole defined by Frank Kermode: "All such plotting presupposes and requires that an end will bestow upon the whole duration and meaning." For a novel to work, you want to come away from reading it with a sense that everything has gathered towards a convincing conclusion— not one that necessarily ties up every loose end, but one that feels an integral part of what has gone before. It must make sense of the space between the beginning and the end. You start reading a novel with no idea where this thing is going to go; you should finish it feeling that it could have gone no other way.

The novelist would like the writing process to be thus; it is not—or at least not for me. I do need to have a good idea where the thing is going—I won't have started at all until a notebook is full of ideas and instructions to myself. And I will have achieved the finishing line only after pursuing various options, wondering if this would work better than that. The reader should have an easy ride at the expense of the writer's accumulated hours of inspiration and rejection and certainty and doubt.

The novelist's problem is infinity of choice. It is also the privilege, of course. Time can be manipulated; so also can the operation of memory. You can make lavish use of it, allowing it to direct what happens, or simply evoke what has once happened in order to flesh out a character, or give added meaning to what a person does or thinks. It is the essential secret weapon, for a novelist. The novel itself occupies a particular framework in time—the period of the action—but there is also the hidden seven-eighths of the iceberg, known only to the novelist, which is everything that went before, that happened to the characters before the story began. In fact, I don't exactly know all of it—rather like personal autobiographical memory, the antechamber of the novel I am writing seems a murky place in which I can rummage around and pounce upon promising fragments: character A can suddenly remember this event, character B can challenge character A by evoking some long-ago behavior. The infinity of choice is at work; I don't actually need to know everything that went before, just the things that are pertinent to the narrative in hand, that may affect it in the way that memory affects real life.

What does memory do to us? It depends on you, of course—what has happened to you, how you are disposed, whether you sublimate, foster, manipulate, reinvent, enjoy, regret, deny, do any of the stuff we all spend time doing. I imagine my own memory behavior is pretty standard. I don't know about the sublimation because I have never been in analysis—the rest is familiar. There are memories that induce shame, guilt, where I wish I could tweak the record—behave differently; there are memories about which I am dubious— maybe I have invented or elaborated this; there are those that I return to, savor, but with a certain melancholy—gone, gone, that moment; there are those that I wish I didn't have. A mixed bag— much what anyone has. Some are highly polished, in frequent use; others are vestigial, surfacing only occasionally, and surprising me. Collectively, they tell me who I am and what has happened to me—or rather, they tell me an essential part of that, leaving much in the mysterious dark cavern of what has been forgotten.

They are in no way chronological, and patently I am not in control of them. They seem to appear of their own volition, and a concerted search for something specific is difficult and often unproductive. Let's try this: a search through my eight decades.

Childhood is at once a challenge, because most memories are among the highly polished, having been summoned up for the memoir I once wrote. But—rooting around—here's a neglected one: I am waiting for Lucy in our favorite garden space where we have a table and chairs. Abdul, the *sufragi*, brings our elevenses on a tray—orange juice and biscuits. I reach for a biscuit. Abdul says, sternly—or seems to say: "Sit!" Puzzled, I sit. Only later does it occur to me that what he was saying was: "Wait for the *sitt*!"—Arabic word for "lady"—I should not start on the biscuits until Lucy arrived.

This memory has its own coda—my realization of a misunderstanding—which is unusual, but rings true: there would have been that childhood fascination with language and its ambiguities. Let's move on to adolescence.

I am staying with my aunt Diana and her family in Kent. Winter 1947, and bitterly—famously—cold. I remember going to bed with all my clothes on. I am fourteen, only recently exiled from Egypt, shunted between my two grandmothers during school holidays because my father is mainly abroad, with a new job. Di has kindly taken me on for Christmas, a somewhat taxing guest, I don't doubt. There is a Boxing Day lunch party to which come friends of theirs, with a son my own age. And he is everything that I am not; he is charmingly forthcoming with adults, charmingly playful with my three young cousins, entirely comfortable with himself—*bien dans son peau*. I am lumpen, too tall, tongue-tied, unable to relate to the children, hideously self-conscious. I observe his performance, and swelter. He ignores me, except for some token charming remarks.

That memory has left me with a lifelong sympathy for adolescence, except that I think they have things rather better now that it is an accepted status. And I was an only child, who had been at a single-sex boarding school. That period was a Calvary; few adults penetrated the miasma of gloom, except for my uncle Oliver, who noticed a reading habit, and talked books to me, and my Somerset grandmother, who simply absorbed me into her routine.

But what about something more upbeat? Something joyous, celebratory, properly young? Trivia float up here: a lipstick called Paint the Town Pink; I am sixteen now and my father does not like me to wear lipstick. He had become a single parent after the divorce, my mother not having applied for custody. He is out at his office all day, so I have put on the lipstick anyway, and sail out feeling glamorous, sophisticated. And, later, at seventeen I think, I have been allowed a pair of wedge-heeled shoes, cutting-edge fashion of the day, and am obsessed with them. The most precious acquisition ever.

Also, around now, my father marries again and I have stepmother number one, Barbara, who has a son of her own, aged twelve, and is perfectly nice to me. We go to Italy for a summer holiday *en famille*, and Barbara has persuaded my father to buy me a sumptuous traveling vanity case for my birthday equipped with little pots of this and that, manicure set, lotions and potions. The sights of Rome I remember not; the vanity case is in my mind's eye to this day. I see now that Barbara was ahead of her time, attuned to the yearnings of a teenage girl. But the marriage lasted only a couple of years, and I never saw her thereafter.

The twenties? Oh, there's plenty here. Marriage, childbirth, becoming a rather young mother. We are in Kensington Registry Office, Jack and I, with our respective witnesses, a friend each, waiting in a somber brown room, occasionally murmuring to one another. An official puts his head round the door and says: "Would you mind making less noise, please?"

I am in the Radcliffe hospital, in Oxford, an emergency admission, having just given birth after a prolonged home labor that went wrong. I am aware that all is not well, because everything is going gray and I cannot speak. A nurse is doing something at a sink, at the far end of the room, but

I cannot attract her attention. The baby is in a crib beside me; she has a little thatch of dark hair. At last, the nurse comes over, inspects me, and at once goes to ring a bell. I hear feet running.

We are off for a weekend excursion in our first car, a Ford Popular. The children are in the back, Adam in a portable bassinet, Josephine alongside (no child seats in those days, or seat belts). We round a bend in a Welsh country lane (somewhere north of Swansea, where Jack has his first academic job), and at the same moment a cow dashes in front of us; we go slap into it. Amazingly, the cow is unhurt; equally, mercifully, all of us. But the car is immovable. The farmer in pursuit of the escaped cow calls for help; the local policeman discovers that Jack's driver's license is out of date but—benignly—decides to take no action: "You people have had enough for one day."

Ordnance survey map in hand, I am making my way across Oxfordshire fields in search of the site of a deserted medieval village. Both children are at school now, and I am free to do this kind of thing, in my thirties—a heady liberation after the child-intensive years. Lapwings lift up ahead of me, and, yes, there are the grassy lumps and bumps of what was once a village called Hampton Gay.

We are driving somewhere in France; a town looms, announced by the road signs—

"Sa cathédrale . . ."—and—"Piscine!" shout the children. The deal is that if we take them to the swimming pool they will then without complaint do time in the cathedral. My next book is going to be a guide to the municipal swimming pools of central and southern France.

Josephine rushes into the house—breathless, distressed: "They're going to drown little black puppies in a bucket!" She has been down at the farm, playing with the three boys there, as on most days. I consider, I take a deep breath, I say: "All right, you can have one." Dogs live for around ten years, I am thinking, Josephine will be eighteen or so and leaving home by then. The puppy was a *mésalliance* between a Jack Russell terrier and a poodle, and lived to be seventeen.

My forties—midlife—and we are into the 1970s now, the age of long cheesecloth skirts (which I wore) and flares (which I did not). These are the Warwick years, when Jack has moved from Oxford to that university. We have come to a poetry reading by Dennis Enright—D. J. Enright—who is Writer in Residence, and we have got to know, and enjoy, him. He starts to read, and after a few moments a young man in the front row of the small audience rises and leaves the room. Dennis breaks off for a moment, sighs: "You win some, you lose some." And continues with the poem.

But there seems to be something awry with this midlife period—the roaring forties, but mine do not roar, they have sunk largely into an oblivion from which Dennis Enright sneaks out. And, yes, here now is a pond in Massachusetts (in England we would call it a small lake) in which I am swimming with my best, my oldest friend, Betty, but a new friend back then, and we are swimming through stripes of hot and cold in this dark green water, and Betty calls: "Look! Look!" and there all around us are large blue dragonflies.

Massachusetts, where I would now go often. The travel years are just beginning, and will fling me hither and thither before long. But for the most part memory is tethered to Oxfordshire, where we live (though in a different elderly farmhouse)—a dim continuous present which sends up occasional images. I am digging over a disused section of the vegetable garden, and am seized with sudden botanical fervor: I decide to take a specific square yard and list every species of plant growing there—hairy bittercress, groundsel, couch grass . . . I am at my desk, working; Jack comes past the window carrying an armful of logs; I hear him open the kitchen door, stamp his wet boots on the mat—thump-thump—drop the logs into the basket . . . Jackdaws have tried to nest in our high seventeenth-century chimney; failing to get their dropped sticks to lodge, they have come down to investigate, and are unable to find their way back, flying around the room and desecrating the furniture . . . There is another mouse in the kitchen trap; I remove it, my pre-breakfast chore. We share this place with much wildlife.

Why do I remember so little about work? These are the work years, also, the early work years. Writing. But that is part of that vague continuous present, until the 1980s—my fifties—when books come to direct my life, determine what I do, where I go.

I am in Docklands, where the skeletal framework of the Canary Wharf buildings are rearing out of a vast and muddy building site. This visit is in the service of the London novel that I am planning, and I have wangled an introduction to an architect working there, who has given me a guided tour, and now points me over to the Marketing Suite. In this sleek reception area, I suspect that my novelist role is not going to cut much ice, and I make some profoundly unconvincing enquiries about office space.

Bicycling in upper Egypt, somewhere outside Luxor, with Jack, and Ann and Anthony. We are on a Nile cruise, disembarked; Anthony has made a sortie into town, and hired the bikes, and now we are spinning on dirt roads through fields of sugarcane and clover, pursued by stray dogs and children. For me, this landscape is at once alien, and entirely familiar. Later, in Cairo, we will discover my childhood home, now part of a teeming suburban slum, but surrounded by such fields, back then.

New Haven, Connecticut. Yale, where Adam is doing postgraduate work. Josephine and I are visiting, and find ourselves taking part alongside him in a civil-rights demonstration. Many of the faculty are on strike in protest against the university's treatment of women and blacks. Adam, who has teaching responsibilities, is on strike, which means he teaches, but not on university premises. We stand in the rain, demonstrating, and Josephine says, rather irritably, that she is not sure this is what she has crossed the Atlantic for.

University College Hospital. Josephine is holding Rachel, who is a day old; she has pink cheeks and a thatch of dark hair. My father appears, in high spirits; he is visiting at the same time this great-granddaughter, and a grandson, Oliver. Nicky, wife of my half-brother Marcus, has also just given birth here. Marcus and his brother Valentine are the sons of my stepmother number two, Daphne. My father—our father—is a wow with the nurses on the ward, who are much entertained by this jovial elderly gent and his complex genetic arrangements.

I wake up, and know at once that I am somewhere else. The birdsong. Outside the window there is birdsong, much birdsong, and it is wonderfully wrong. It is song such as I have never heard before. In fact, I am in Australia, at an idyllic country motel to which the long-haul participants in the Adelaide Literary Festival have been brought to detox after their flights, before the festival begins. I open the window, listen some more, see birds I cannot begin to identify, and realize that I am seeing and hearing that Darwin was right. This is another continent, where things are done differently.

We are into the 1990s here, and I have hit sixty. I don't remember feeling especially bothered about this—full of energy still, writing, living. The view from eighty says: huh! a mere slip of a girl—just you wait.

Slovenia. I have been sent by the British Council to British Book Week at Ljubljana. I am being briefed on the day's activities over breakfast by the British Council representative when one of the Slovenian officials rushes up to cry excitedly: "Your Mrs.Thatcher is fallen! She is no longer the government, she is gone!" We say: "Oh! Great!" It seems to me now that the Council representative was a touch out of order here, with such openly expressed political commitment. "You will need to go home," continues the Slovenian. "You will need to be with your families. There will be . . . disorder." We say that no, we don't need to, and there won't be, and recognize the gulf between those who have lived always in a politically stable society and those who have not.

And I have to note here the curious conflict between what is remembered and what was taken down at the time, for a diarist. Wanting to check this exchange, I looked in the diary: nothing about it at all, nothing. But several pages on other aspects of that week that only returned, vaguely, as I read. The conference on contemporary British fiction, for example, at which, apparently, papers were delivered on such subjects as "The Macedonian response to the Movement poets," and 'The Serbo-Croat reception of the Sirens episode in *Ulysses*." Really? However can I have forgotten that?

In fact, a short story eventually surfaced from that time—"The Slovenian Giantess"—and the diary entries had come in useful here, along with that other, unrecorded, memory. That, essentially, is what it has been for, the diary. And, at the time of writing the story, in 1994, I was apparently bothered about "the inexplicable shift between significance at the time and significance in recollection—the way in which memory evidently transmutes events . . . Now if you could lay a finger on why one moment is immortalized and another obliterated you would presumably have made a seminal discovery about the workings of the human mind . . . All a fiction writer can do is take note." I quite agree, eighteen years on.

Recent memory—the last ten or fifteen years— seems reasonably well furnished. More grounded— less travel now—and much that is distressing: death, illness. The hospital years, Gore Vidal has called this period of life, and yes, indeed, there is plenty of hospital experience—Jack's, my own. Verdicts delivered by kindly, deliberate, consultants: "We have a problem;" waiting rooms; procedures; trolley rides to operating theaters, contemplating the building's internal pipework overhead; the unrelenting hospital pillow; "How is your pain today—on a scale of ten?"

But much else, too. Isaac says: "When you're four, *Horrible Histories* is good, but you don't really understand it. When you're five, you understand it but it isn't so funny." He is five—Adam's fourth child, and my sixth grandchild. We have gone forth and multiplied.

Luxborough village fête with Josephine. There is to be a hawk and falconry display, but the hawks and falcons refuse to fly; they sit glowering on the grass, or on the handler's wrist. He points out the reason—a pair of buzzards circling overhead: "My birds are saying no way are they going up there with the local thugs around." We repair to the produce tent, for cakes and chutneys; it is heaving in there, it is Harrods sale.

Monksilver village fête. There are camel rides on offer, the camels a discordant sight against the tipping green hillsides of west Somerset. I win an extremely ugly teapot in the raffle.

Old Cleeve village fête. Minehead brass band is playing, and I send Adam a photo from my newly acquired mobile phone, proud of this techno-logical achievement.

The village fête years also, evidently. Forget Australian literary festivals, Toronto Harbourfront, Chicago. And that is just fine. Nowhere have I been happier, more fulfilled, than in west Somerset.

But these are essentially the London years, where I am ending up, rather to my surprise—I am not at heart a city dweller, but it makes every sense: family, above all.

The banshee wail of police-car sirens. The yellow-white night sky, jeweled here and there with a creeping airplane. City snow—a brief miracle, disheveled within hours. The subterranean past, glimpsed when I spot the stem of a clay pipe in a mound of soil thrown up by road works.

I am a bus person; I hate the tube. The spiderweb of the London bus system has hardly changed in sixty years; the 73 performs today exactly as it did when I was very young. One day a few years ago, I was on an Islington bus whose novice driver mistook the route and plunged off down a tree-hung road. Branches snapped off and cascaded down. The driver was heard to wail: ". . . I don't know where to bloody go!" A local lady rose and stationed herself beside him— brisk, authoritative, one of those natural crisis containers—and delivered crisp directions until we were back on course.

Minicab drivers have been an education: Turkish, Kosovan, Afghan, Iranian, Iraqi, Polish,

Estonian, Albanian—these disparate people converging on London, resourceful, opportunist, often wanting to talk, and giving me in a half-hour drive an insight into lives flung around by circumstance. On the Holloway Road, an Iranian says: "My father was a university professor. I am an economist. Now . . ." He shrugs, lifting his hands from the wheel.

City life: alone, and in a crowd. Just me and the book I'm reading, of an evening; within a few hundred yards there are dozens, hundreds of people, but I wouldn't know it. Passing the British Library, I see from the bus a face I know, a friend, and this familiarity—this personal resonance—is startling amid the anonymity all around.

City life: today, and a whole lot of yesterdays. I cross my own path, time and again—walk up the steps of the British Museum, and there is my own alter ego, doing the same, ten, twenty years ago. I meet myself at a particular seat on the Embankment, in Bunhill Fields, at the Soane Museum, in Tavistock Square—and remember what I was doing, who I was with. The city is collective memory, and every kind of personal refrain, for anyone. You are rich, in the city. Maybe not such a bad place in which to end up, after all.

So there it is—the random search through eight decades. There is selection here, obviously. But not a selection that I have mulled over, sorted with care. And there is no pattern that I can see, no particular revelation. This is just a trawl from the mass of lurking material, the moments that I have, that I have had for years. There are many, many others, of course; some I prefer not to share, others are so tattered, so incidental, that they would make no sense to anyone else. And others so prosaic, so dull, that they seem to have no content. This lot just looked like some of the more presentable.

We can make a choice from accessible memories, as I have just done, but we can't choose what to remember, and what not to remember. There is something disturbing about the thought that, if some other, hitherto unavailable retrieval system were activated, I might find myself with a series of entirely unfamiliar memories—an alternative past that happened, but of which I had ceased to be aware. I suspect that I am straying into the realm of analysis here, but I am looking at the idea more from a novelistic point of view, and while it is disturbing it is also fertile matter for fiction. A fictional character is equipped with a past that establishes and defines them, just as I am, and you are. But suppose that past—those memories—were to be supplanted by a different set; what then would happen to the personality concerned? I am conditioned by—cushioned by— what I remember, which tells me what has happened, or what I believe to have happened, and how I have behaved, or think I behaved. Pull the rug away, furnish me with a whole new set of memories which make things look rather different, which make me see myself differently, and what will happen to me? Do I go mad? Or emerge as someone else, a revised personality?

This is a fancy; for me, a possible prompt for a story, even a novel. A new way of exploring the significance of memory in fictional terms. But it is a meaningful fancy, too, because it points up the power—the defining power—of the memories that we have. We are who we are because we have that particular range of memories, which form our past as we know it.

When I pinch the leaves of the rosemary plant in my garden, and sniff, I am back on a hillside above Jerusalem, aged nine. I suppose there must have been wild rosemary there. This is an instance of what psychologists call the "Proust phenomenon," in reference to the novelist and that now overworked madeleine. Smells, tastes, are famous memory prompts. Psychologists find olfactory memory interesting because there is an argument about whether the Proust phenom-enon—smell and taste as memory triggers—exists at all, and if so whether it is always laid down in early life, and accessed best in later life. In old age the ability to distinguish smells is apparently much diminished, which may have something to do with it; back once more to the heightened response to the physical world when you are young. But in that case the distinctions are preserved: rosemary takes me back to the Jerusalem hillside, thyme and marjoram do not.

There is a sensuality about memory, then. And the heritage industry seems to have latched on to this idea. A London pub-cum-restaurant cultivating a nineteenth-century atmosphere used to smell authentically of coal fires, despite being centrally heated throughout and free of such things; an aerosol spray was available, apparently—canned nostalgia. And at Jorvik, York's re-creation of the Viking town, to which you can return in a trolleycar that trundles back through the centuries and past scenes of Viking domestic and commercial life, the sights and sounds are augmented by pungent whiffs of livestock, cooking, and inadequate sanitation. The past can be conjured up by the appropriate aroma, much as supermarkets seek to induce a spending appetite with the smell of newly baked bread, and house agents urge us to woo prospective buyers with a waft of fresh coffee.

But it is not that memory is scented, rather—if the Proust phenomenon exists—that smells evoke a time, a place. That moment has not gone, can be recovered, because an experience in the present brings it back; my London garden is tenuously linked to what was in 1942 a Palestinian hillside.

This is the sense in which memory is the mind's triumph over time. The same has been said of history, and I relish both concepts: it is as though individually and collectively, we succeed in seizing hold of what is no longer there, that which should be unavailable, and making it miraculously permanent and accessible because it matters so much, because we need it.

We are robust about time, linguistically, we are positively cavalier about it—we make it, we spend it, we have it, we find it, we serve it, we mark it. Last time, next time, in time, half-time—one of the most flexible words going, one of the most reached for, a concept for all purposes. Time is of the essence, or it is quality, or time will tell. We talk about it . . . all the time, I find myself writing. There. But when I think about time, I am awed. I am more afraid of time than of death—its inexorability, its infinitude. It is as unthinkable as space—another word we tame by making every use of it. And in old age I am time made manifest; sitting here, writing this on a summer afternoon, twelve minutes past three, the watch hand moving relentlessly round, my weathered body is the physical demonstration of passing time, of the fact that eighty years have had their way with it, that I ain't what I used to be. I have lived with time, in time, in this particular stretch of time, but before too long time will dump me; it has far to go, and we don't keep up with it. None of us, ever.

Fifteen minutes past three.

Impersonal, indifferent; it neither knows nor cares. It sweeps us along, the ever-rolling stream and all that, nothing to be done about it, but we do have this one majestic, sustaining weapon, this small triumph over time—memory. We know where we have been in time, and not only do we know, but we can go back, revisit. When I was nine, I was on a Palestinian hillside, smelling rosemary (and collecting a wild tortoise, but that is another story). Time itself may be inexorable, indifferent, but we can personalize our own little segment: this is where I was, this is what I did.

Reading and Writing

My house is full of books. I suppose that I have read all of them, bar reference books and poetry collections in which I will not have read every poem. I have forgotten many, indeed most. At some point, I have emptied each of these into that insatiable vessel, the mind, and they are now lost somewhere within. If I reopen a book, there is recognition—oh yes, I've been here—but to have the contents again, familiar, new-minted, I would have to read right through. What happens to all this information, this inferno of language? Where does it go? Much, apparently, becomes irretrievable sediment; a fair amount, the significant amount, becomes that essential part of us— what we know and understand and think about above and beyond our own immediate concerns. It has become the life of the mind. What we have read makes us what we are—quite as much as what we have experienced and where we have been and who we have known. To read is to experience.

I can measure out my life in books. They stand along the way like signposts: the moments of absorption and empathy and direction and enlightenment and sheer pleasure. Back in the mists of very early reading there is Beatrix Potter, who does not just tell an enthralling story but challenges the ear. Her cadences, her linguistic flights that I repeated to myself over and over: "The dignity and repose of the tea party," "too much lettuce is soporific," "roasted grasshopper with ladybird sauce," "The dinner was of eight courses, not much of anything, but truly elegant." When eventually I came to write for children myself, an occasional pursy-lipped teacher would tell me that I sometimes used words that a seven/eight/ten-year-old would not know and I should stop it. Such letters were thrown out—beneath contempt; go and read Miss Potter, lady.

Later, much later, I met up with Arthur Ransome and was transported to an alien world in which unimaginably liberated children larked around in boats in some exotic landscape of hills and greenery and water. I was growing up in Egypt, and had known nowhere else; I would surface from *Swallows and Amazons* to my own mundane backdrop of palm trees, a string of camels beyond the garden hedge, the postman's donkey titupping up our drive.

That Egyptian childhood was book-heavy. I did not go to school, but books made me. I have written elsewhere, in a memoir of those Egypt years—*Oleander, Jacaranda*—of my home instruction, the Parents' National Educational Union system devised for expatriate families and administered, in my case, by someone who had herself left school at sixteen. That was education, and I am concerned here with books in a rather different sense. But there is an overlap, inevitably. The Do-It-Yourself education method was focused entirely upon reading: the child was read to, required to "tell back," and in due course to read and "write back"—a sustained exercise in the absorption of language. I am grateful to it. The Bible—the King James Version, of course—featured strongly. Palgrave's *Golden Treasury of Verse*. And, above all, for me, Andrew Lang's *Tales of Troy and Greece*, that late Victorian retelling of Homer. The *Iliad* and the *Odyssey* spilled out of lesson time into the rest of the day; I reenacted the siege, the wanderings, as I drifted around our garden, because of course I was in there anyway—Penelope—so this must be something to do with me personally. The solipsism of the nine-year-old mind. Except that I was in there with the wrong part; Penelope is not as beautiful as Helen, she is described as wise and good, qualities that did not appeal. And Ulysses—red-haired and crafty—is clearly not a patch on brave Hector or glamorous Achilles. So I juggled with the narrative—true to the tradition of reworking Homer, had I known it—airbrushed the tiresome Helen, and set myself up with Achilles. And, to bring things more up to date, equipped him with an infantry tank and a machine gun, instead of all that stuff with chariots and spears—the Libyan campaign was raging a hundred miles or so away, remember, in 1941.

Many of the books sent out from England by the PNEU failed to reach us. We fell back on our own resources, for reading matter. Dickens's *Nicholas Nickleby* and *David Copperfield*—immersed in the drama and tragedy of mysterious lives, reading as literary innocents, barely aware that the setting was the nineteenth century. Macaulay's *Lays of Ancient Rome*, with me learning great chunks by heart: "Lars Porsena of Clusium, by the nine gods he swore . . ." I did much learning by heart, and some of it lingers, surfacing at unexpected moments, a shred of Tennyson, a whisper of Shelley: "Break, break, break/On thy cold grey stones, O sea." "Swiftly walk over the western wave, spirit of night." Deeply out of educational fashion now, learning by rote, but it was hanging on still when I did eventually go to school, aged twelve, and I accumulated more: Shakespeare speeches, Wordsworth, Keats—bits and pieces of which I still have and I wish there were more still. You can only learn by heart when young, unless, I suppose, you are an actor.

I think I was probably starved of fact—of non-fiction. The educational system's offerings were not enticing: Plutarch's *Lives*, and a turgid book on the history of Parliament which serviced the weekly period known as Citizenship Studies. I did relish our Natural History text, Arabella Buckley's *Eyes and No Eyes*, published in 1901, so not exactly up to date, and dealing with the flora and fauna of Devon—entirely inappropriate to our Nile-fed garden, but with its own exotic and vaguely scholarly charm. This paucity of fact may account for my passion for Hendrik Van Loon's *The Home of Mankind*—a treasured possession that still has a place on my shelves. When I open it now there is a whiff of that long-ago appeal; it is a nicely eccentric geography book with chatty text and the author's own pungent views to the fore: "Poland suffers from two great natural disadvantages. Its geographic position is most unfortunate, and its nearest neighbours are its fellow-Slavs of Russia." And the illustrations are a delight: the author's own quirky drawings, accentuating geographical features. He demonstrates watery Europe, fringed by its elaborate coastline, invaded by chunky rivers; if the Pacific ocean should run dry—with the land-masses perched on top of peaks; the Atlantic—a section of blue underwater mountains with a curved surface on which perch tiny ships.

By the time I arrived in England I was thoroughly book-addicted; socially inept, after that isolated upbringing, a floundering outcast at the fearful boarding school to which I was dispatched, but an ace reader. Books became my retreat—anything, everything. My school holidays were spent going from one grandmother to the other. My London grandmother's Harley Street home was well equipped with books—short on creature comforts, in the late 1940s, but plenty to read, though reading that required a degree of perseverance.

I plowed my way through Charlotte M. Yonge—*The Dove in the Eagle's Nest*, *The Chaplet of Pearls*, *The Daisy Chain*—and Harrison Ainsworth—*Old Saint Paul's*, *The Tower of London*, *Windsor Castle*. I cite these not as signposts along the way—I was reading what was available, not what I would have chosen—but as indicators of what a desperate adolescent reader will undertake if necessary. Charlotte M. Yonge seems to me now an extraordinary challenge for a mid-twentieth-century thirteen/fourteen-year-old—those long, dense, mannered historical novels. In her own day, she had published many of them in serial form in her *Monthly Packet*, which one commentator has called the first teenage magazine. Victorian adolescents must have been made of stern stuff. Commentary on Charlotte Yonge is something of an industry. There is a Charlotte Mary Yonge Fellowship, which holds regular meetings and publishes a twice-yearly *Review*, and indeed the writer herself was an industry, with about one hundred and eighty works to her name, mostly novels. And she was highly regarded by her peers—George Eliot,

Gladstone, Tennyson, Trollope. But not much read today, except by the stalwarts of the Charlotte Mary Yonge Fellowship. I have several of her novels, 1880s editions but evidently not filched from my grandmother's shelves because they bear penciled secondhand bookshop prices—35p, 25p. So I must have acquired them in adult life, out of nostalgia, maybe.

William Harrison Ainsworth is an equally unlikely choice—but of course this was not really choice, it was a question of what was available in that high, chill, Harley Street house, where the main rooms had all been dust-sheeted for the duration of the war, and the books stared darkly out from within glass cases. Harrison Ainsworth was another prolific Victorian—thirty-nine novels, master of the popular historical romance, friend of Dickens in their early writing lives. I think I enjoyed him rather more than Charlotte Yonge; there is a memory of being fascinated by the atmosphere and action of *Old Saint Paul's* and *The Tower of London*, which probably chimed with a nascent interest in the presence of the past, its visible evidence—I would have been taken to both sites by my grandmother.

Where choice operated, I discovered Mazo de la Roche, Canadian author of the Jalna novels, and wallowed in this family saga—rich with romance and spiced with lurking sex. And there was a brief, alarming engagement with the London Library.

The uncle who had observed my bookish tendency gave me temporary membership for a sixteenth birthday present—my first experience of a great library. You could order books there, back then; for some obscure reason I ordered Hakluyt's *Voyages Round the World*. It arrived on a cart, in several volumes, and I sat stolidly reading for a week, unable to admit to a mistake.

At my Somerset grandmother's house there were fewer books, but there was a complete run of bound volumes of *Punch* from about 1890; many a long, bored afternoon was spent poring over one of these, mainly in pursuit of the cartoons, but sometimes tackling the text, and picking up something along the way about the social attitudes of the early twentieth century and what seemed the heavy-handed humor of the day. There was little fiction; I moved on from Charlotte Yonge to Charles Morgan (boring), A. J. Cronin (ditto), and other popular novelists of the twenties and thirties.

At last, a few years later, I plunged into the public library system and unfettered reading. Oxford Public Library, where the poet Elizabeth Jennings worked, and stamped your chosen books, and I observed her with awe—a few years older than me and a writer, a poet at that. And then the small branch library in Swansea, where Jack had his first permanent academic post at the university. I was coping first with a toddler, and then a three-year-old and a baby, and would trundle both in the pram to the library once a week, packing Iris Murdoch, Graham Greene, Evelyn Waugh around them for the return journey. It was not the best time at which to be servicing a reading addiction; I remember reading in snatches while feeding the baby, shoveling food into an infant mouth, minding them in the park or on the beach.

Early reading is serendipitous, and rightly so. Gloriously so. Libraries favor serendipity, invite it; the roaming along a shelf, eyeing an unfamiliar name, taking this down, then that—oh, who's this? Never heard of her—give her a go? That is where, and how, you learn affinity and rejection. You find out what you like by exploring what you do not. In the late 1940s, when I was first putting a toe into the waters of real grown-up books, the favored authors of the day were the Sitwells— Edith, Osbert and Sacheverell (just to recite their names brings back the mocking refrain of a disrespectful number in some late-night revue less doting than the reading public)—Norman Douglas, Lesley Blanch, the kind of writing that did not use one word where ten would do—florid, self-conscious, portentous. I read dutifully and thought that either the times were out of joint or I was. And then later, much later, I found Henry Green and Ivy Compton-Burnett, and realized that what I was after was economy and accuracy, the use of that just right, but startling language. Henry James and Elizabeth Bowen taught me that writing can be expansive and complex but still be accurate and exciting. I had no thoughts then of writing myself—I was reading purely as a gourmet reader, refining taste, exploring the possibilities. And now I think that a writer's reading experience does not so much determine how they will write, as what they feel about writing; you do not want to write like the person you admire, even if you were capable of it—you want to do justice to the very activity, you want to give it your own best, whatever that may be. A standard has been set.

The signposts sent me toward particular kinds of writing; these were what I wanted to read and, when eventually I came to write myself, these would be—not how I wanted to write but the majestic exemplars always in the back of my mind. But no one—writer or otherwise—reads in search of stylistic satisfaction alone; what is said matters just as much as how it is said. Where fiction was concerned, I had the basic needs of any fiction reader—I wanted to escape the prison of my own mind, my own experience, and discover how it may be for others, to see other people's lives distilled through an author's imagination. The variety, the disparity, of fiction, is a constant astonishment. How can it be that there is such abundant fertility—that so many

174

people turn to and create character, and narrative—both extraordinarily difficult feats, as anyone knows who has tried to do it. Well, only a very few do it with real power and effect, of course. But many, many have a shot at it—even more so today, with universities up and down the land offering their Creative Writing MA courses, so that it begins to seem as though you need formal qualifications to become a novelist. My generation beavered away in solitude—whether for better or for worse, I wouldn't care to say.

Sixty years or so of fiction reading now, for me. A torrent of story poured in, much of it forgotten entirely, a good deal half remembered, some so significant that I go back again and again. I have had fitful relationships with some writers. At one time I could no longer read Lawrence Durrell; now, suddenly, he is again alluring. I can't abide Barbara Pym—enjoyed her once. Anthony Powell is irritating today, yet in the past I have reveled in Widmerpool and company. And there is the handful with whom each rereading is a new discovery. William Golding, who offers something you hadn't noticed before each time you go back, in every single book of his. Updike, Henry James, Willa Cather, Edith Wharton . . . others.

The stimulus of old-age reading is the realization that taste and response do not atrophy: you are always finding yourself enthusiastic about something you had not expected to like, warming to some writer hitherto right off the radar. But, that said, there is by now that medicine chest of works to which you return time and again. And, if I had to whittle that down from a chest to a slim stash—the desert island books—there are three titles that I would pick, because, for me, they are perhaps the ones that have most elegantly demonstrated what the novel can do, when the form is pushed to its limits. And these are: Henry James's *What Maisie Knew*, William Golding's *The Inheritors*, Ford Madox Ford's *The Good Soldier*.

What Maisie Knew is a brilliant exercise in narrative technique, in which an entire tale of adult betrayal and duplicity is seen through the uncomprehending eyes of a child, a fictional discussion of evil and innocence in which the reader is eerily and uncomfortably aligned with the forces of darkness because recognizing the corruption which the child's vision simply records without the insight of experience. *The Inheritors* is a novel of ideas in which the ideas and the discussion of human nature are so effectively subsumed within the story that each new reading of it points up another layer, or shifts the emphasis. It is also the saddest novel I know. And *The Good Soldier* is another marvelous narrative tour de force in which the truth behind a pattern of relationships is revealed with such subtlety and guile that while the reader is never deliberately deceived, each new release of information changes the view of what has happened. All of these are books in which the apparently straightforward business of telling a story about some characters has been refined to its most delicate and allusive but at the same time to its most powerful. You are left with a feeling of astonishment, and of involvement, because part of the skill has been to draw the reader into the book, to make the reader a participant by inviting judgment and complicity. The reader becomes a confidant, as it were, and, like a confidant, may find that there has been an ambivalence. You are left with an insight into human behavior, into your own.

Just as importantly, the signposts were starting to wave where nonfiction was concerned—they were dancing up and down, indeed. They pointed me toward landscape history, toward archaeology. "Oh, there's a book you'd like . . ." said Jack one day, offhand—he was an academic political theorist, by trade, but seemed to have read everything and anything—". . . W. G. Hoskins— *The Making of the English Landscape*." I read, and my way of seeing the world was changed. *The Making of the English Landscape* was first published in 1955; I read it in around 1965, when we were living in Church Hanborough, a few miles outside Oxford. I devoured the book, put on my rain boots and walked out in search of ridge and furrow, lost medieval villages, drove roads—all of which could be found within a radius of ten miles or so. Hoskins makes you see the physical landscape as a palimpsest, layers of time inviting interpretation; he lets you see it also as a challenging medley, where everything exists at once—today, yesterday and long ago all juxtaposed. For me, this vision was to become a driver for fiction—the presence of the past, whether in an Oxfordshire field or in someone's life. We are all of us palimpsests; we carry the past around, it comes surging up whether or not we want it, it is an albatross, and a crutch.

The Hoskins approach to landscape history has come under criticism as "Romantic"—harking back to the Wordsworthian tradition of landscape appreciation—and also too heavily weighted in favor of historical evidence rather than the archaeological record. The New Archaeology of the 1950s—processual archaeology—considered that the survival of a landscape in the present cannot and should not be used to infer past processes: Hoskins's interpretations had sometimes done precisely this. That said, those working in the field who have reservations about his approach readily admit that he has been an inspiration, to them and to many others.

"You might try Norman Cohn—*The Pursuit of the Millennium*," said Jack. "And Frances Yates—*The Art of Memory*." I did, I did. I was finding the kind of history that had not been on offer during my three undergraduate years at Oxford. Not that I am ungrateful for that induction; those three years created a climate of mind, I am certain—they did not make me into a novelist but they determined the kind of novels that I would eventually write. But now, through with Stubbs Charters and the *Oxford History of England*, I could spread wings, discover different history. In 1971 Keith Thomas published his magisterial *Religion and the Decline of Magic*. I was enthralled—here was the history I had been wanting, without knowing that I did. And there was more of it around: Peter Laslett, Christopher Hill, Alan Macfarlane. Jack had been a historian as an undergraduate, but had focused on the history of ideas for his postgraduate work, and thence became a political theorist. He had been unfashionable on the history scene, in the early 1950s, when the Namier school still dominated—the insistence that the course of events is directed by politics and personalities. But the Namierites and their study of ruling elites were soon to be shunted aside in favor of social history, the emphasis on people and how they have lived, behaved and thought. And, where Jack was concerned, the history of ideas had come in from the cold.

Subsequent reading—the reading of a lifetime—has been this marriage of the fortuitous and the deliberate, with the random, the maverick choices tipping the scale and serving up, invariably, the prompts for what would next be written. Books begetting books; intertextuality, of a kind. It has never felt like that—more that something read has sparked off a story idea that is owed to that subject but will eventually have nothing much to do with it. But if I had not read that book, the story might never have arrived, or not in that particular form. Elizabeth Bowen, whom I admire and regularly reread—no falling in and out of favor there—has a short story called "Mysterious Kor" in which a pair of lovers wander the nighttime streets of blitzed London. Years after writing it, she herself wrote that her description of that moonlit, ruined cityscape must have been prompted, subliminally, by a memory of reading Rider Haggard's *She* in childhood—the eerie, imagined city in that novel. In that instance, a half-forgotten reading experience inspired and informed a story, decades later.

It has not been fiction so much, for me, but the random discoveries. Sometime in the 1970s I came across William Stukeley, probably in Stuart Piggott's biography; Stukeley, along with my abiding fascination with archaeology, would inspire *Treasures of Time*, a novel concerned indeed with archaeology, but that is also a love story and a take on the attitudes of the 1970s, and the title came of course from Sir Thomas

Browne's *Urne-Buriall*—"The treasures of time lie high, in Urnes, Coynes and Monuments . . . ," a text that Jack had pointed me toward, long before, something that he had read in his voracious teenage reading years and returned to whenever he wanted to remind himself of the glories of seventeenth-century English prose-writing.

A decade or so later, the popular science writing of the day brought me Stephen Jay Gould's *Wonderful Life* and the lightning struck once more; his account of the Cambrian fossils of the Burgess Shale, most of them evolutionary dead-ends except for the one from which we are descended, was the fuel for a novel about the apposition between choice and contingency, *Cleopatra's Sister*. A while later, the chance acquisition in Toronto's Royal Ontario Museum of a booklet about Martin Frobisher, the Elizabethan seaman, would be the trigger for a London novel, *City of the Mind*, a novel about time and the eloquence of place—and a further love story. And, later still, a rereading of Frances Yates's *The Art of Memory* made me see how I could make a house—my grandmother's house—speak for the century by way of its contents, a piece of nonfiction this time: *A House Unlocked*.

None of these books would have been written, or written in the way that they were, if I had not come across something that in some mysterious symbiosis inspired and wound in with what I was already thinking about, in a vague and inconclusive way. These readings lit a fuse. And from the point when first I recognized what was happening I have known that I have to read—mostly undirected, unstructured reading. Those of us who write fiction write out of much—out of what we have seen, and done, and heard, and thought, out of every aspect of experience—but as far as I am concerned books are a central part of that experience, the driver, quite as much as my own life as lived, with all its inevitable limitations and restrictions.

These have been books that were prompts, that triggered work of my own. But when I look along the nonfiction shelves there leaps to the eye a collection of titles that seem to be saying something about a need, a taste—no, something more than that, a pursuit, a cultivated hunger. They are fingered, reread. Here is Barry Lopez's *Arctic Dreams*, Hugh Brody's *The Other Side of Eden* and *Maps and Dreams*. And Colin Turnbull's *The Forest People* and *The Mountain People*, equally reading-worn. What are the Arctic and the Congo to me? Travel books? But these are not travel books; there is indeed a travel section, but these are something apart, with something in common. There is Peter Matthiessen's *The Snow Leopard*, and everything by Robert Macfarlane, and a row of Redmond O'Hanlon titles.

These books complement some adventurous streak in me? No. Rather, the opposite. I am not adventurous; I have enjoyed travel, but of the most cushioned kind. I relish the physical world, and liked to walk it, when the going was good, but knew only the well-trodden ways of my own country—Exmoor, the South Downs, Offa's Dyke. What these books and their like have done for me is tap into some roaming tendency of the mind; I know that I could never have done what these writers have done, been where they have been, pursued the interests they have pursued, but I want to know what it is like. We go to fiction to extend experience, to get beyond our own. For me, this kind of nonfiction writer is furnishing the same need—taking me out of my own comfortable expectations and showing me how it might be elsewhere. Armchair travel? Not quite. I have never believed that travel broadens the mind, having known some well-traveled minds that were nicely atrophied. Rather, these are books—experiences—that encourage a leap of the imagination. Hugh Brody invites you into the life of the Inuit; Barry Lopez offers a glimpse of the Arctic, richer and more vivid by far than any television documentary. Colin Turnbull is describing existence at its most harsh, in Africa, and is also showing you human nature. Redmond O'Hanlon—well, I would be alarmed to go for a walk along the Thames towpath with Redmond

O'Hanlon but I want to go with him vicariously up the Amazon, or to the Congo, or Borneo, or the North Atlantic. Equally, Robert Macfarlane takes me to the places I could never have known, and sets me off on all manner of inquiry in the process. And from where I am today, in the tiresome holding-pen of old age, that seems all the more valuable.

My Somerset grandmother—to whom I was devoted—had reservations about reading as an activity. Definitely not in the morning: "You should be out and about, my dear, not sitting there with a book." Possibly after tea, a more relaxed time of day, but in moderation, always: "You'll ruin your eyesight." This was in the late 1940s, when Aldous Huxley's method of treating poor eyesight was much in fashion. My London grandmother was keen on that; I was made to sit for a quarter of an hour twice a day, elbows on a cushion placed on a table in front of me and the heels of my palms pressed lightly against my eyes. You were supposed to "think black." I had been wearing glasses since I was seven, but Huxley was apparently nearly blind, so one was tempted to say that the system clearly hadn't done him much good.

One-sixth of the world's population is myopic, but amongst readers the proportion is much higher—about a quarter. Habitual readers, that is—those who spend much time reading. Which raises the intriguing question of whether we book-addicted are thus because of some genetic conditioning or whether we have wrecked our eyesight through our addiction, as my grandmother would have claimed. Whichever, we are in distinguished company—Aristotle, Goethe, Keats, Wordsworth, Joyce. Samuel Johnson, shown in that iconic portrait both peering at a book and abusing it, wrenching the pages round the spine.

The ophthalmologist and writer Patrick Trevor-Roper looked at the way in which myopia may have affected writers and artists, citing as an instance the images in the poetry of Keats and of Shelley: short-sighted Keats often favored auditory subjects—the "Ode to a Nightingale," the sonnet "On the Grasshopper and Cricket"—and his images tend to be within his focal range: the Grecian urn, the "beaded bubbles winking at the brim," whereas Shelley, who had no sight problem, went in for the distant prospects of sky and mountain. And there is an identifiable myopic personality, it seems: myopic children don't flourish in the playground or at sports—they can't see what's going on and they miss the ball; but reading and writing are not a problem—within their field of vision—so they focus on that and tend to do better academically than their peers, though they may not be more intelligent.

In the past, to be seriously myopic must have been crippling; you would have had problems with all daily activities, many trades would have been out of the question. And who ever heard of a myopic warrior? As for hunter-gathering, forget it. Today, we are well taken care of, with contact lenses and varifocals and competing high-street optometrists. Even the adage of my youth has rather lost its clout: "Men seldom make passes at girls who wear glasses." I gather they do, nowadays.

Myopia is a human disability; there are no myopic animals, except for some instances in domesticated dogs. And this makes perfect sense; natural selection would account for that—a short-sighted bird of prey wouldn't last long. So is a myopic hunter-gatherer conceivable? Common sense suggests not—the tendency would have been bred out, if it appeared. And this seems to be right; myopia is indeed a relatively modern condition. If so, why? Was my grandmother on the case, with her suspicion of reading?

Opinion is against her, it seems. A classic study of a hunter-gatherer society—an Inuit group—found a very low level of myopia among older members who had lived the traditional isolated lifestyle but a far higher level among their children who had grown up in a Westernized community and had received schooling. At first the finger was pointed at books, until it was realized that the older Inuit group had always done close work in ill-lit igloos—the making and repair of clothes and weapons. Other studies of hunter-gatherer communities have confirmed this onset of myopia with the advent of Western dietary habits, and this is now thought by some to be the explanation: carbohydrates. The cereals and sugars that are the basis of modern diet but unfamiliar to those accustomed to high levels of proteins and fats. An excess of carbohydrates can affect the development of the eyeball, causing myopia. As for those myopic domesticated dogs: dog biscuits?

So myopia is not genetic? I look around my own family, in which specs and contact lenses are rife, and doubts creep in. Surely there is something going on here? Patrick Trevor-Roper certainly thought there was, in his study, homing in on the Medicis; one Medici pope is on record in a portrait holding a concave lens, an early form of glasses, while other Medicis are referred to as having bad sight, and "beautiful large eyes"; the myopic eyeball is large. Also, their dynastic success was based not on soldiery but on banking, scholarship and the encouragement of art—a nice display of the myopic personality. But it seems that there is as yet no identification of a specific gene responsible for the short-sightedness that appears to be endemic in some families; the favored conclusion at the moment is that a combination of genetic predisposition and environmental factors stimulates the development of myopia. Your parentage may well have something to do with your life behind specs; equally, your circumstances—if you grew up with the emphasis on study rather than long-distance running. Reading may play a role, but is far from being the whole story. Myopia is a modern trend, but owed probably more to the availability of sugars and cereals than to universal education. Books are excused—for the moment, and up to a point.

But books and specs go together, no question. At the dire boarding school to which I went, where one of the punishments was to spend an hour in the library, reading (there wasn't anything much in the library, except for some battered reference books), the myopic amongst us were labelled "brainy," a term of abuse. And we were probably bad at games too, a further social solecism. Ah! The myopic personality. Reading was seen as something you did only when you had to, an attitude connived at by the staff. My copy of *The Oxford Book of English Verse* was confiscated from my locker: "You are here to be taught that sort of thing, Penelope. And your lacrosse performance is abysmal."

I broke out into the clear blue air of higher education, eventually, and a lifetime of unfettered reading. And yes, my sight is pretty dodgy—

cataracts and macular degeneration—but the splendid specialist who will do his best to ensure that I don't lose it further exonerates the books: I would have headed that way in any case.

Reading, for all of us, is fettered only by obvious restrictions. You can't own all that you want or need to read. There are, then, two kinds of books—yours, and the contents of libraries. There is the actual, personal library, your own shelves, which mark out reading inclinations, decade by decade, and the virtual library in the head—the floating assemblage of fragments and images and impressions and information half-remembered that forms the climate of the mind, the distillation of reading experiences that makes each of us what we are.

Let's look first at the actual library—the real, tangible books. My two thousand plus, which is nothing very much in personal library terms and requires no cataloging system beyond crude subject allocations: fiction in the kitchen, poetry in the television room, some history upstairs, other history down. Alberto Manguel, in his lovely book *The Library at Night*, says: "Every library is autobiographical . . . our books will bear witness for or against us, our books reflect who we are and what we have been . . . What makes a library a reflection of its owner is not merely the choice of titles themselves, but the mesh of associations implied in the choice." His own library sounds awesome: many thousands of books in a converted barn somewhere in France, the amazing accretion that is the fruit of his tastes, his eclectic reading, his generous interest, his voracious curiosity. And his book is a homage to the very concept of the library.

My granddaughter Rachel, at the age of ten, was made library monitor for her form at school. She had all the proper librarian instincts; under her aegis, the form-room books were arranged by subject matter, and, within that, in alphabetical order. She was away ill for a week and came back to find that some interfering ignoramus had reshelved everything in height order; Rachel was outraged, quite rightly.

Had she known of it, she would have no doubt attempted an embryonic Dewey system. So would I—had I the time and the energy and rather more books than I have. When I was first raiding the public library system, I didn't know what those cryptic numbers on the spines meant, and was entranced when at last enlightened—the elegant simplicity of the Decimal Classification system whereby the field of human knowledge is divided, and then subdivided—theoretically ad infinitum. Dewey is under fire these days, it seems, but I still like the elegance.

Alberto Manguel does not use Dewey, it would seem; his library has "no authoritarian catalogue" and the title of his book—*The Library at Night*—is intended to evoke that random, disordered quality that he feels so crucial to a library, that power to make connections, create echoes, cross cultures. A majestic collection such as his would do precisely that; it has the discipline of groupings, in some form, and further groupings within these, but its essential feature is that it is a private not a public library. The shelving system of a public library must be apparent to all users; a private library is *sui generis*—it has been assembled in response to the pursuits of a particular mind, a particular reading life, and is colored by all the associations and connections of that particular reading narrative. It is not trying to be comprehensive; it is relishing selection. It is about time and space; it tells you where this person has been, in every sense. Manguel records his pleasure, when unpacking his books and starting to arrange them in their French barn, at the coded references he found among the pages: the tram ticket reminding him of Buenos Aires, the paper napkin from the Café de Flore, the name and phone number scribbled on a flyleaf.

Exactly so. For any of us, with our humbler collections, the books have this archival aspect; they are themselves, but they also speak for us, for this owner, for you, for me. My books spill train tickets, invoices, pages of notes, the occasional underlining or swipe with the highlighter (though

I don't approve of defacing books). A little copy of *Silas Marner* in a slipcase has my name in childish handwriting—Penelope Low—and a year, 1945. And there too is the printed sticker of the bookseller: Librairie Cité du Livre, 2 rue Fouad, Alexandrie. So I acquired it at the age of twelve, in wartime Alexandria. And it has followed me from there, and then.

Perhaps my most treasured shelves are those with the old blue Pelicans, over fifty paperbacks, including some seminal titles: F. R. Leavis's *The Great Tradition*, Margaret Mead's *Growing Up in New Guinea*, Richard Hoggart's *The Uses of Literacy*, Richard Titmuss's *The Gift Relationship*. And John Bowlby's *Child Care and the Growth of Love*, which had us young mothers of the midcentury in a fever of guilt if we handed our young children over to someone else for longer than an hour or so lest we risked raising a social psychopath—even the father was considered an inadequate stand-in. Pelicans were the thinking person's library—for 3 shillings and 6 pence you opened the mind a little further. And Penguin had of course their own flamboyant Dewey system— the splendid color-coding: orange for fiction, green for crime, dark blue for biography, cherry red for travel.

I don't have enough old Penguins. The Pelicans have survived, but the rest have mostly disappeared—read until in bits, perhaps, or left on beaches or in trains or loaned and not returned. And long gone are the days when a paperback meant a Penguin, pure and simple, let alone when a paperback publisher could confidently market a product with no image at all on the cover—just the title and the author's name, emphatically lettered. Beautiful.

Biography and autobiography and memoir are alphabetical by subject, for me, and I rather relish the strange juxtapositions—Edith Sitwell and Wole Soyinka, Kipling and Werner Heisenberg. Like a game of Consequences: He Said To Her . . . And The Consequence Was . . . This is Manguel's library at night—the library of thoughts and voices and associations. I was once taken on a tour of the stack at the Humanities Research Center in Austin, Texas, where the long shelves of that great literary archive reach away into shadowy distances, each run of boxes labeled—Hemingway, Joyce, Woolf—and one imagined it when the archivists were gone, a silent colloquy of all those voices.

The biblical story of the Tower of Babel has an apparently malevolent Deity creating a confusion of languages in order to foil attempts at the unity of mankind, the term Babel thus becoming a synonym for linguistic chaos. A library is indeed a Tower of Babel—multilingual, multicultural. Jorge Luis Borges was a librarian as well as a writer, a dual commitment which presumably accounts for that enigmatic story "The Library of Babel" in which he proposes a library that is composed of infinite hexagonal galleries, in which each book is of uniform format—four hundred and ten pages—and among which librarians wander in interminable pursuit of some final truth, the book that will explain all books, many of whom have strangled one another, succumbed to disease, or committed suicide. It sounds more like life as lived than the ambience of the British Library, the Library of Congress or the Bibliothèque Nationale and indeed the story can be read as some sort of fable or allegory with the library as the universe: "unlimited and cyclical." But the image is a powerful one: the multiplicity of a library, the cacophony of voices, its impenetrability, unless you can read the codes. When I worked in the Round Reading Room at the British Museum, before the British Library moved to St. Pancras, I used to have a fantasy—a short story that I never wrote—in which humanity has disappeared, all systems are down, forever, and members of an alien race pad into the Reading Room, taking down the catalog with their long green fingers, crack teams of scholars who have been set to work to penetrate the mysteries of this inexplicable archive, in which, now, all material is of equal significance: the Lindisfarne Gospels and *Beekeeping for Beginners*, the Koran and the *Guinness Book of Records*, *Hamlet* and *Asterix*. A great library is anything and everything. It is not for its current custodians to judge what the future will find to be of importance, and it is this eclecticism that gives it the mystique, that is the wonder of it. A private collection is another matter entirely: you or I have accumulated what we feel to be of significance to us, the books speak for what we have responded to or wanted to know about or got interested in and may include many acquisitions that have sneaked in for no good reason, like—in my case—that fat hardback *Collected Works* of Jane Bowles, whose work I do not care for, and plenty of other titles toward which I am indifferent but that I might need to check out at some point.

There has been plenty of checking out in the service of these pages. That is the other function of a private library—reference. Today we have the Internet, and very wonderful it is, and I am getting better at Googling, but an atavistic urge still has me reaching for the Shorter Oxford, or Chambers, or *Brewer's Dictionary of Phrase and Fable*, or *The Oxford Dictionary of Quotations*, those reliable companions over the decades.

My first engagement with a great library was as a student. A vague memory of induction to the Bodleian is that it involved making some kind of ritual declaration in Latin—presumably that you wouldn't steal or abuse the books—and of the inimitable smell of Duke Humfrey's Library, the rich aroma of old book—very old book, in that case. I doubt if I ever went into it again. The Radcliffe Camera was the place for history undergraduates; you got to know it all too well, homing in on favorite desks, from which you could look around and see who else was there, the hunt along the shelves for the book you needed and the frustration when you found it was already taken, which meant a search for the reader and a negotiation about how long he or she would be wanting it. One man always achieved the book I was after before I could get to it by dint of arriving at the library the moment it opened, which I never managed to do. Years later I came across him again, by which time he was the distinguished historian Theodore Zeldin; it was somehow gratifying to know that he had put the books to better use than I had—one forgave that preemptive early rising.

In 1993 I was invited to serve on the Board of the British Library, and did so for six years, only too glad to give up some time and energy to an institution from which I had had so much. And what can be more important than the national archive? Here is the record of pretty much everything that has been thought, and said, and done over the centuries, not just in these islands but the world over—the Library thinks multicultural, it reaches out in space as well as time. As a reader, I was awed by the sense of that vasty deep from which you could conjure up not spirits, but the precise work you had noted in the catalog, the sense of infinity of choice but also of order imposed, the idea of an immeasurable resource, a grand ideal, made available to individual inquiry. As a Board member, I was immersed, involved, sometimes baffled, occasionally panic-stricken.

Membership of the Board was quite a commitment: ten meetings a year of three hours or so, each meeting served by a batch of papers that certainly took me half a day or more to read. Some ancillary commitments. Board membership carried a modest salary; you had been appointed by the secretary of state. In my day there were, I think, twelve members, who included the three senior executives of the Library. Eleven suits, and me; for three years I was the only woman on the Board. The sole advantage of that, from my point of view, was that my isolation made it virtually impossible for the chairman to avoid my eye if I wished to say something: discrimination, that would have been.

I enjoyed those Board years—learning corporate speak, a language new to me, watching the St. Pancras building rise from the rubble of its construction site, for this was the point at which the Library was about to leave its old home in the British Museum. We had conducted tours, wearing hard hats, being briefed about the problems with wiring and shelving. It was a dismaying process at times; you thought you had signed up for involvement with the running of a great library, instead we found ourselves presiding over the travails of one of the most elaborate and complex construction processes this country has known. There was plenty of white water— boardroom confrontations between our project manager and that of the Department of Arts and Libraries, responsible for the construction, angry letters flying from the Library to the Department. I listened to civil service speak, also new to me. But at last the new Library was there. I remember a triumphant completion tour: the acreage of shelving, the marvels of the book delivery system, the light-flooded reading-rooms. The safety measures: the sprinkler system, the steel doors that would close in the event of fire. One of these was demonstrated—the imposing shutter that inched slowly and remorselessly down. And I remember that Matthew Farrer, a fellow Board member, looked at me and we both said "Gagool!"—being of the generation that read *King Solomon's Mines*. A neat instance of cultural community, and nicely appropriate to the Library.

The technologies of today were relatively new, back then, but the Library was at the cutting edge. Turning the Pages became available, that enthralling process whereby you can wipe a finger across a screen and leaf your way through a virtual Luttrell Psalter or Sherborne Missal. The then director of information technology gave a presentation on current innovations, and was asked by someone what he thought the most significant information development so far. Without hesitation he replied: "The book—user-friendly, portable, requires no infrastructure, relatively non-degradable."

Since then, the e-book. I don't care to read on an e-reader myself, though I would under certain circumstances—when traveling, or if in the hospital—and I get bored by the exclusive defense of either paper or screen. Future readers will require both, I assume, but I can't imagine that many would wish to own a personal library that consisted of the Kindle on the coffee table, rather than some shelves of books, with all their eloquence about where we have been and who we are.

There is a devastating poem by Tony Harrison about his mother's death, about love and grief, about the distance between him and his father:

> Back in our silences and sullen looks,
> for all the Scotch we drink, what's still between's
> not the thirty or so years, but books, books, books.

I can hardly bear to read that poem; it is so sad, and so true. Books can have a divisive power.

They can estrange—but can also unite, of course. Great courtship material, books—that discovery of a shared enthusiasm, the exchange of gifts. We read to bond, to oblige, to discover how someone else reads. And read to persuade, to agree or disagree. Why weren't book groups around when I was a child-tethered young mother in Swansea in the 1960s? Why didn't we think of starting one up? They are a marvelous concept, combining a social and intellectual function: you spend time with like-minded others. You read something you might not otherwise have read and are provoked to defend, or criticize.

Cultural community is shared reading, the references and images that you and I both know. Books are the mind's ballast, for so many of us—the cargo that makes us what we are, a freight that is ephemeral and indelible, half-forgotten but leaving an imprint. They are nutrition, too. My old-age fear is not being able to read—the worst deprivation. Or no longer having my books around me: the familiar, eclectic, explanatory assemblage that hitches me to the wide world, that has freed me from the prison of myself, that has helped me to think, and to write.

Six Things

My house has many *things,* too, besides those books—the accretions of a lifetime. Not many of them are valuable; some of them are eloquent. People's possessions speak of them: they are resonant and betraying and reflective. When house-hunting, I used to find myself paying more attention to the furnishings than to the house one was supposed to be inspecting. They spoke of the people who lived here.

So in this last section I have picked out six of the things that articulate something of who I am. This is to plagiarize myself, in a way—I used a similar device in *A House Unlocked*, making objects in my grandmother's house speak for a time, for the century. But self-plagiarization seems to me permissible. And, at this late point in life, I have seen these objects in the house imbued with new significance—I have seen how they reflect interests, and concerns, how they chart where I've been, and how I've been.

I imagine them in an estate sale, or an auction room, mute, anonymous, though perhaps each might be picked up, considered, thought to have some intrinsic merit—or not. The bronze cat would be a snip—someone would bag that. The

Jerusalem Bible might appeal, and the sampler. The leaping fish sherd and the ammonites and the duck kettle-holders are probably in a box of assorted junk, unwanted.

But before that happens let me give them each their story—theirs and mine. A sort of material memoir.

The duck kettle-holders from Maine

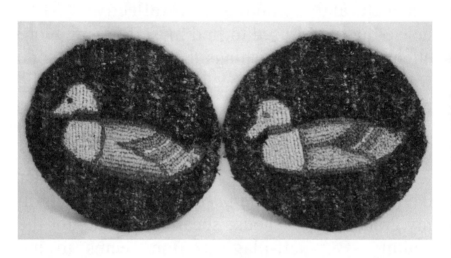

These are, strictly speaking, American folk art. They are a pair of circular kettle-holders, about nine inches in diameter, each with a duck worked in colored wools on sacking. They were sent me by my friend Betty, many years ago, as an addition to our collection of emblematic ducks which had accrued—inevitably—when we lived in Oxfordshire at the seventeenth-century farm-house called Duck End. Decoy ducks, gift shop ducks, small oriental papier-mâché ducks.

These particular ducks had been made by an old lady living at some rather remote spot in Maine; she made such things for sale at local fairs and was working nicely in the American folk art tradition. The ducks are closely woven in wool, simple, stylized, and with their markings picked out in different colors. Betty breeds border collies and is a renowned sheepdog handler and demonstrator at sheepdog trials. She was on a trip to one such trial up in Maine, had rather lost her way and was in desperate need of water for her dogs. She stopped off at the old lady's house to ask for water and directions. The old lady invited her into her kitchen, filled a can, and Betty spotted the ducks and exclaimed. It was apparent that this was by way of a (very small) business, and she asked if she could buy them. The old lady demurred: trouble was, she needed something for the craft fair next week, she was right out of burlap so couldn't make some more, and if she let these go she would have nothing to show. Okay, said Betty, what if I drive to a store, get you some burlap—then could I have them? That would be fine, it seemed. So Betty sought the nearest store (some way away), achieved a yard of sacking, and the ducks were hers. And, in due course, mine.

The ducks are stitched on a mottled gray-brown background, and outlined in blue. They have brownish-buff sides, a blue band at the tail end, with some white, cream-white head and breast, short beak and rounded head. Precisely portrayed ducks. And it seems to me that this lady who had lived all her life in rural Maine, amid its wildlife, would not have adorned her kettle-holders with any old made-up duck. These would be some actual duck. So—I must turn to Peterson—*A Field Guide to the Birds East of the Rockies*.

American Peterson is lavish, compared to our own familiar European Peterson. We have five owls (British, that is—we can't claim European exotics such as Tengmalm's owl); they have twelve, and that's east of the Rockies only. Eleven woodpeckers for heaven's sake, as against our own mere three. A whole page of what we call "little brown jobs": Confusing Fall Warblers. You can say that again—they look more like Indistinguishable Fall Warblers to me. And a whole squad of them, when we have only to deal with chiffchaffs and garden warblers and the willow warbler and a few more.

But what about my ducks? There is nothing in Peterson that exactly corresponds, but the harlequin duck is not a bad fit. The harlequin duck has brown sides, glimpses of blue at the tail and is described as a "smallish slaty duck with chestnut sides and odd white patches and spots." And—aha!—the range is right and the habitat is described as "tumbled mountain streams, rocky coastal waters." Plenty of rocky coast where Betty was driving. So I choose to think that the kettle-holder ducks are the old lady's personal take on the harlequin duck. And she worked them in the fine tradition of American folk art, probably just as her own mother and grandmother had done.

I have a copy of American Peterson because for as long as I can remember I have bird-watched, in the most amateur way possible, just if and when an opportunity arose. I have a *Field Guide to the Birds of Australia* as well, and I sometimes take that up just to browse in wonder among its esoteric offerings: helmeted friarbird, Australian king parrot, flame robin. And to remember the morning a kindly couple of ornithologists in Adelaide took me to a salt-marsh bird sanctuary: pelican, egrets, ibis, storks. And the rosellas in suburban gardens, the flocks of sulphur-crested cockatoos in the bush, the tiny sapphire wren I once saw. Australian bird-watching made our own homely collection seem tame indeed.

So the Maine ducks tap into a lifelong fringe interest, for me. I always notice birds. A small triumph when I have spotted egrets in the Exe Estuary from the train, going to a literary festival. Keeping an eye out for red kites over the Berkshire Downs, driving to Somerset with Josephine. Looking for the pair of jays that sometimes appear in my London square. And, time was, I kept the Official Duck End Bird List beside my desk in Oxfordshire; species seen as I worked there. The rule being that the bird must have been seen as I sat, without getting up. Around thirty, I think, including treecreeper, nuthatch, all three woodpeckers, flycatcher, all the tits. I can't think how I got any work done.

In Orkney, once, we had the experience of being taken to a sea-bird cliff on Papa Westray by the young woman ornithologist whose summer job was to record the success or failure of the nesting birds—a daily record, with each nest site plotted on transparent paper laid over photographs of the cliff. The populations to be thus assessed, and whether stable or falling. The cliff face was a tenement, its assorted occupants at different levels—fulmars, razorbills, guillemots, kitti-wakes . . . And other treats in Orkney, flagship of the Royal Society for the Protection of Birds: an outing with Eric Meek, its area manager there, who would indicate a speck on the far side of a loch—"and there's a female merganser," pick out a hen harrier amid a distant flock of gulls, stare at something bobbing about invisibly in some reeds—"A phalarope!" The real ornithologist sees with enhanced vision; they speak another language. But the rest of us can potter about on the nursery slopes, finding out.

What is it about birds? The Royal Society for the Protection of Birds' current membership stands at over one million, topped only by the National Trust. Is it that they are ubiquitous—town or country? That we have been educated by television nature programs? That we recognize the last gasp of the dinosaurs? Perhaps that bird-watching as an activity costs little—unless you insist on some state-of-the-art telescope—can be done almost anywhere, including out of your own window. Garden bird-feeders are national suburban equipment, and apparently make a significant contribution to the survival of some species. Suffice it that many people respond to birds, more than to any other creature. I once stood watching a pair of pied wagtails on a railway platform—you don't so often find wagtails making a living at a train station. They were largely ignored, and then I noticed a woman intent upon the birds; we exchanged little conspiratorial smiles: "You too!"

I have never seen a harlequin duck, and I don't expect I ever shall. But somewhere there is one foraging on a rocky coast, tenuously linked to the kettle-holders in my kitchen.

The blue lias ammonites

Fossils. Two little curled shapes, an inch across, that hang in the gray ocean of a sea-smoothed flat pebble of blue lias, itself just larger than an opened hand. I picked it up on the beach at Charmouth, in Dorset, long ago. I have other ammonites—exquisite polished sections, but bought from the fossil shop at Lyme Regis, which

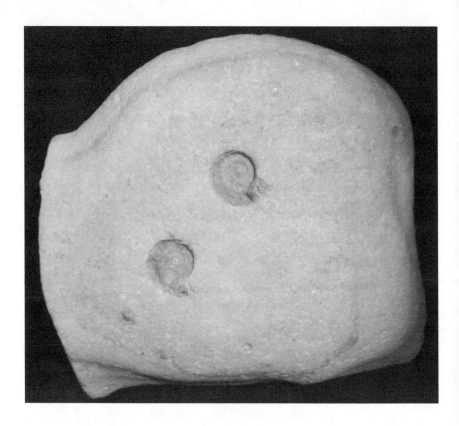

is not nearly as satisfying as the one you found yourself. They amaze me, these small creatures that expired together once, in just such proximity, I suppose, so many million years ago, and remain thus, propped on my bookshelf.

Between one hundred and ninety-five and two hundred million years ago, since the blue lias is late Triassic and early Jurassic, the seam of rock that runs down across the country from Yorkshire to the south coast at Dorset, taking in north Somerset and parts of south Wales. Ammonites are marine invertebrates, and, quite apart from their own immense antiquity, their very name races back through time, owed to Pliny, who called these fossils "horns of Ammon" because their spiral shape resembled tightly coiled rams' horns, associated with the Egyptian god Ammon. It is like the night sky being named for Greek mythology—Andromeda, Cassiopeia, Aquarius, Orion, Pegasus—the physical world demanding a much deeper reference than our own small slice of time.

Ammonites lived in open water, for the most part, cruising in ancient seas, myriads of them, falling on their death to the sea floor where they were gradually buried in the accumulating sediment. The ammonoids show rapid evolution; species evolve and become extinct at faster rates than other groups, making them useful index fossils, used to date the sedimentary rock in which they are found. Our own Jurassic ammonites seldom exceed nine inches in diameter—my two are mere babies at an inch. But there was a German monster over six feet across and others in North America at four feet, while the Portland stone here can offer a two-foot species.

Ammonite taxonomy is vast—there were masses of them, evolving, becoming extinct. Because of where they were and when, my two in their little slab of blue lias must be some kind of asteroceras or promicroceras, but it is impossible to tell which, or what they were within their genus—*Asteroceras confusum* (is that a joke?),

Asteroceras stellare, Promicroceras pyritosum— goodness knows.

Paleontology is awe-inspiring, sobering. Deep time. It puts you in your place—a mere flicker of life in the scheme of things. I take note of that whenever I walk on one of the north Somerset beaches. The blue lias surfaces here, lifting out of the Bristol Channel—the gray and pink pebbles at Watchet, the cliffs seamed with equally gray and pink alabaster. My aunt Rachel used the alabaster for sculpting, foraging for chunks at the foot of the cliffs after winter storms. It was tiresome material to sculpt—too soft, too liable to crumble under her tools—but we have two of her successes, a long, gray, rather primeval-looking fish, a relative of the coelacanth, I'd say. And a little maquette, a Henry Moore figurine. I've often picked up ammonites at Watchet, both embedded in a stone or as an isolated snail shape. Belemnites, too, those pointed tubular forms. In fact, I think it was on Watchet beach that the deep past first signaled, when I was ammonite-hunting as a teenager.

Ammonites and a paleontologist have surfaced in fiction, for me—an instance of the way in which the things that alert the mind then insert themselves into what gets written. Shape it, indeed. Watchet beach and its ammonites some-how prompted a novel in which the central figure is a paleontologist, whose career trajectory begins when as a child he heaves up a lump of blue lias at Watchet, and sees something intriguing upon it. I don't think I would have made much of a paleontologist myself—I don't have a sufficiently scientific turn of mind; he is a surrogate, perhaps. And, for a novelist, it is the accumulation of all these matters grabbing the attention over the years that will direct the sort of stories that get told, the kind of people who will inhabit them. Every aspect of time, for me, from the deep time of the ammonites through the historian's attempt to analyze the past, to the bewildering operation of memory.

But rocks and fossils never seem like putative material, at the time—they are just something that has made the mind sit up and pay attention. I wish I had paid attention more systematically—done some rock-watching in the way that I have bird-watched, and checked what I was looking at. The blue lias is all that I can recognize, and Devon's red sandstone, and Oxfordshire's oolitic lime-stone, which built two of the houses in which I have lived. The regrets of old age are polarized: you wish you had not done certain things— behaved thus, responded like that—and you wish you had seized more of the day, been greedier, packed more in. I wish I had packed in more rocks—on foot, legging it, learning what it was I walked over, looked at. Walking was a central pleasure, time was—Offa's Dyke, when the going was good, Wenlock Edge, a bit of the Pennine Way. I looked up, and around—birds, wild-flowers—but didn't focus on down, on the deep time over which one was walking.

The naming of things. I have always needed that, where the physical world is concerned; much poring over bird books and my forty-year-old copy of Keble Martin's *The Concise British Flora in Colour*. It annoys me that I can't identify my blue lias ammonites; just "some kind of asteroceras or promicroceras" won't do. The world and its life are the abiding delight and fascination, and to savor them to the full you want to have things labeled, named, classified; a tree is not just a tree, it is a particular tree, or you are only enjoying it as an agreeable sight. I can understand exactly what drove Linnaeus, despite being myself quite unscientific. Taxonomy is crucial, essential—the majestic discipline that marshals the natural world, so that everyone can know what is what and what it is not. Perhaps this urge for identification began for me in the nursery in Egypt (it never did get known as the schoolroom) when Lucy and I did Natural History on Wednesday mornings out of Arabella Buckley's *Eyes and No Eyes*, that late-nineteenth-century guide to the flora and fauna of the English pond and stream: caddis fly larva, water boatman, dragonfly. And, indeed, out of Bentham and Hooker, the standard wildflower manual; we searched the fringes of the sugar-cane fields for scarlet pimpernel, shepherd's purse, vetch.

The Jerusalem Bible

It is New Testament only, quite small—about nine inches by five—and it is bound with exquisitely inlaid mother-of-pearl, making it feel heavy, chunky. This must be real mother-of-pearl. If it were a tourist offering of today, I would propose plastic imitation, but plastic was not around in 1942, so it must be the real thing, ripped probably from the floor of the Red Sea, and this is therefore an environmentally reprehensible Bible. But environmental concern was not much around either in 1942.

Lucy bought it for me at the Church of the Holy Sepulchre in Jerusalem, and has written in it: Penelope Low from Nanny. It was late summer 1942, when Rommel's army in Libya had advanced to within a hundred miles of the Egyptian border, and British families were advised to leave the country. My mother had opted for Palestine, as opposed to Cape Town, the alternative; my father stayed at his job with an Egyptian bank. This would be only a temporary interruption to the status quo, seems to have been the assumption, we would soon be going home— as was indeed the case, but the bland optimism now seems strange: it looks today as though Egypt could very well have fallen to the German advance, and must have done so at the time to anyone facing the facts.

The title page of the Jerusalem Bible says, at the foot: "The American Colony Stores, Jerusalem, Palestine." I am sure that this means simply that it was produced for this outlet, which presumably then supplied some bookstall at the Holy Sepulchre, because I am certain that Lucy's purchase took place there. More on the American colony in a moment; for now, we are in the crowded, incense-reeking interior of the church, and somewhere in a crevice of memory that day lingers, this carefully considered purchase—which would have been quite expensive, and I was grateful, and proud of this new treasure—and Lucy's prickly response to this place: its clamor, its rituals, the smells and bells, the mass of people. She had good reason; Lucy was paid-up Church of England, and the Church of the Holy Sepulchre was everything but that. This was a long way from the measured sobriety of Cairo's Anglican Cathedral. The Church of the Holy Sepulchre is—was—the headquarters of the Greek Orthodox Patriarch, and control of the building is shared between several churches—Roman Catholic, Eastern and Oriental Orthodoxies. Anglican and Protestant Christians have no permanent presence. Lucy was feeling herself to be on alien territory, and was probably bothered about this because she was quite devout, and this after all was the site of Golgotha, where the Crucifixion took place, and where Christ was buried. Perhaps the purchase of the Bible was a small defiant statement: we too are Christians.

And it must have caught the eye. It is handsome—on the front a Greek cross, set in a circle within a diamond of mother-of-pearl inlay, further small inlay slabs all around, forming a nest of rectangles, the whole thing iridescent—a shimmer of blues, pinks, greens, pearly whites. Mother-of-pearl; nacre.

Nacre is the inner shell layer of some mollusks, long valued as a decorative material—all those billions of pearl buttons, for starters. I have a butter knife with a mother-of-pearl handle; many such were manufactured during the last two and three centuries, no doubt. But nowadays the species supplying this industry are endangered, and plundering the oceans in the service of buttons and knives is frowned on. That shop in Covent Garden that used to have baskets stacked high with giant shells and nacre mollusks has long since closed down.

So, thus, that morning in 1942, and the Bible that remembers the Church of the Holy Sepulchre (and, at one remove, the vibrant life at the bottom of the Red Sea). We were there as tourists, and must have seen its sights, but of those I remember nothing. I was nine.

Hadrian built a temple on the site, originally—the temple of Aphrodite—which was demolished by the Emperor Constantine in around 325 when he had required his mother, Helena, to build churches on all the sites associated with the life of Christ. Helena is said to have discovered the True Cross during her excavations, though it is not clear whether it was under her auspices that it eventually got broken up into relics that would provide churches everywhere with enough fragments to marshal a whole army of crosses. The medieval relics marketing industry is fascinating: ideally, a splinter of the True Cross, or a Holy Thorn, failing that, hair or toenail of a saint, even a more substantial chunk of bone. Christ is of course the problem, there never having been an available corpse; but never mind, that can be got round, with a bit of ingenuity: a phial containing the breath of Christ. A religious tourist trade that has diminished today to Bibles and postcards.

Constantine's edifice was built as two connected churches, most of which were destroyed in 1009 by the Fatimid caliph, though in a later deal between the Fatimids and the Byzantine Empire some rebuilding was allowed and a mosque reopened in Constantinople. Then came the Crusades; the objective of every Crusader was to pray in the Church of the Holy Sepulchre. Jerusalem was taken, and throughout the Crusader period there was much rebuilding and excavation of the church and its site, until the city fell to Saladin in 1184, though a treaty allowed Christian pilgrims to enter the church. Effectively, the site was a battle-ground for centuries, the building itself rising and falling, knocked down, restored, revived, neglected, fought over. And, it appears, this tradition survives with occasional brawls between the contemporary occupants; in 2002 the Ethiopian contingent objected to a Coptic monk having moved his chair from an agreed spot—eleven people were hospitalized after the resulting commotion.

Representatives of all these sects would have been there on that morning in 1942—Greek Orthodox in full fig, monks and priests and a herd of tourists that would have included plenty of those displaced by the war, like ourselves. Soldiers everywhere, and RAF and ATS and WAAF; we were connoisseurs of categories and uniforms—some Aussies over there, and those are New Zealanders, and he's Free French. Jerusalem would have been a favorite leave destination.

Lucy and I were living in some style. We were at Government House, by invitation of the British High Commissioner's wife, because before Lucy took me on she had looked after their children. And thus it was, there, that I saw General de Gaulle in his dressing-gown, but that too is another story. My mother had not been invited to Government House, and was staying more modestly at the American Colony Hotel, which I remember as having a lovely courtyard with orange trees, resident tortoises, and amazing ice cream. It was the hotel of choice for the discriminating: charming, cheap, more select than the cosmopolitan and pricey King David, and with an interesting background.

The hotel was run by descendants of an American religious group. I gave an inaccurate description of these in *Oleander, Jacaranda*, drawing on remembered hearsay. I am now better informed. They had left Chicago for Jerusalem in

1881, so as to be there well in time for the Second Coming at the millennium. They were joined by others from America and from Sweden, and eventually formed a community of a hundred or so, who engaged in good works, diversified into farming, and, after the Second Coming failed to take place, the surviving family of the original group founded the hotel, sited partly in the historic "Big House" just east of the Damascus Gate which the first arrivals had made their home. There my mother stayed, modestly, and there could I, today, though rather less modestly.

The American Colony Hotel is five star, now, and when I Google it I can indeed see a garden courtyard, and very inviting it looks. "Privately owned boutique hotel . . . an oasis of timeless elegance." Swimming pool, complimentary Internet access, TV with in-house video. And there is obliging availability: I can have a standard double room tomorrow night for £175, or—if I want to push out the boat—the Deluxe Pasha King Room for £345. Are there still tortoises, I wonder? And do they still produce Bibles bound in mother-of-pearl?

I have four more Bibles, as well as the Jerusalem Bible. So I am an agnostic who owns five Bibles. One is the battered old King James Version with which I grew up, from which Lucy and I read every morning at the start of the day's lessons: Bible Study. Then there is something called the Bible Designed to be Read as Literature, which seems to bestow literary status on the original text simply by knocking out the traditional verse numbers. Given to me by my grandmother. And then there is a dreadful thing called the Good News Bible, which has little cartoony illustrations and has debased the language of the King James Version to such an extent that I shall not even give a quote, to spare those of you who have not come across it. And there is a further offering called the New International Version, which is somewhat less debased but why bother at all, when you have the King James? These last two were acquired by myself, when I noticed them in churches I was visiting—Pevsner in hand, usually—and thought: what on earth is going on?

The language of the King James Version was laid down in my mind, as a child, like some kind of rich sediment: those cadences, the rhythm of the phrases. The fact that we met unfamiliar words and that meaning was occasionally obscure bothered neither Lucy nor me. Lucy was there for reasons of piety and the requirements of the National Parents Educational Union's daily timetable; I rather enjoyed the stories. Intensive exposure to that beautiful text, to the liturgy, to the narrative, has not made me a Christian, evidently, but I am profoundly grateful for it. If you don't know something of the biblical narrative you are going to be bewildered by most early art and by innumerable references in English prose and poetry. And if you have not known the King James Version you will not have experienced the English language at its most elegant, its most eloquent.

I am an agnostic who relishes the equipment of Christianity: its mythologies, its buildings, its ceremonies, its music, the whole edifice without which ours would be a diminished world. I like to attend a service. I am a church-visiting addict, with cathedrals the ultimate indulgence. An ambiguous position; some may say, hypocritical. I want it all to go on, I want it all to be there, but I can't subscribe to the beliefs. I am accredited—baptized, confirmed; but nobody asked me if I wanted to be, at some point skepticism struck, and I stepped aside. But not very far; there remains a confusing, or confused, relationship with this physical and mythological presence, which is in some way sustaining. Perhaps this is because I grew up with the Bible and the rituals of the Church of England; perhaps it is because, however secular-minded, you can recognize the effect, the allure of religion (which is why I call myself an agnostic rather than an atheist). Jack shared my unbelief. A friend and colleague of his, Father Conor Martin, was a Jesuit priest, a fellow political theorist and an academic in Dublin; Conor perfectly accepted Jack's position, but had also his own subversive comment: "Ah, but Jack, you're a spiritual man." I think I know what he meant.

The Gayer-Anderson cat

It is seated upright, seventeen inches tall, an improbable cat in that its front legs are unrealistically long, but otherwise entirely catlike, sinuous, elegant, prick-eared, its back legs invisible beneath its haunches, its tail lying straight alongside. It has a powerful presence—its cavernous eye sockets seem to stare enigmatically. It wears gilt earrings and a nose-ring, a silver necklet, and there is a winged scarab on its chest and another on its forehead.

The original is a familiar presence in the Egyptian hall of the British Museum. Mine is a replica, sold by the Museum's shop and a Christmas present from Jack over twenty years ago. The shop still sells them, online, for £450. Not as much, I trust, back then. The cat is a representation of the cat goddess Bastet, likely to have been a votive statue, and dates from what Egyptologists call the Late Period—about 664–332 BC. For the Museum, it is one of its most iconic objects, much viewed and admired, and, as I write, I learn from the Internet that it is on loan this year to the Shetland Museum at Lerwick. You can't get much further than that from ancient Egypt.

The cat was given to the Museum by Major R. G. Gayer-Anderson, who had collected it in Egypt in the 1930s along with much else by way of Egyptian antiquities—7,500 items of all periods were given to the Fitzwilliam in Cambridge by him and his twin brother. A sizeable haul, back in the days when scooping up antiquities from Egyptian traders was a favorite activity of foreign visitors. Today, removal of antiquities is strictly forbidden; you can't—or shouldn't—smuggle out so much as a potsherd.

Gayer-Anderson acquired the cat from a dealer and went to work on it to get rid of the accumulated surface incrustations, and to repair some of the damage it had suffered. His repairs seem to have been reasonably skillful but the cleaning process rather too enthusiastic; the original surface is now lost, and its present appearance—that gleaming greenish-black—is not what it would have been when it was created.

Gayer-Anderson was a friend of my London grandparents, and family legend has it that when he came back to England after his long residence in Egypt he loaned the cat to my grandmother for a while before giving it to the Museum, and it formed the centerpiece of her dining-room table at 76 Harley Street (my grandfather had been a surgeon in the days when such medical people owned an entire Harley Street house, and brought up their families there).

I wonder if this is true. Neal Spencer, in his booklet for the Museum on the cat, gives an account of its movements after it arrived in England which makes the family story somewhat unlikely, on the face of it. The cat seems to have spent the late 1930s and the war period in a sealed wooden box in the vault of Lloyds Bank in Lavenham, Suffolk, while a lady called Mary Stout, a friend of Gayer-Anderson and temporary custodian of the cat, argued with the Museum about the terms of the bequest. But . . . it is possible; there may have been some interlude when it ended up with my grandmother—she was certainly also a close friend, and this legend must have sprung from somewhere.

By the time I came to that house, in 1945, the cat was gone—if ever it was there—and Gayer-Anderson had died. But I had met him as a child, in Egypt, when my mother and I were occasionally invited to tea at the Bayt al-Kritiliya, the restored seventeenth-century Mameluke house in old Cairo where he lived and which he had made a sort of Arabian Nights incarnate with its fountains, mashrabiya windows, oriental furnishings. The tea served was conventional English afternoon tea, but the rest was exotic, magical; I adored it. Alas, of Gayer-Anderson Pasha (the honorific bestowed on him by King Farouk) I remember little. Large, jolly—that is the impression.

He had lived in Egypt for many years, having been seconded to the Egyptian army from the Royal Army Medical Corps after training as a doctor. There, he became Egyptian Recruiting Officer, and, later, Oriental Secretary to the High Commission—the British High Commission in Cairo, that is. This must mean some kind of adviser, I suppose—the man who knows a lot about how things operate around here. Gayer-

Anderson probably did, and described himself as an Orientalist—that now somewhat discredited term. He contributed to a memoir of my Harley Street surgeon grandfather, and described their initial meeting at Gallipoli in 1915, on the Base Depot Ship *Aragon*, over a dinner with "many a good yarn capped by a better." My grandfather was notoriously genial, and a raconteur, and they clearly hit it off, all amid the carnage of the Gallipoli campaign, with my grandfather honing his surgical skills when not breaking off for a convivial evening.

They met up again a bit later in Cairo, where Gayer-Anderson showed my grandfather around and described him as "unfailingly courteous and considerate" toward Egyptians of all classes "as is not always the case with Europeans." I'm rather pleased to hear that, and I note Gayer-Anderson's implied disapproval of the prevailing attitudes of the day; he was only too right, and it was much the same twenty years or so later, when I was growing up there.

So what does the Gayer-Anderson cat mean to me, staring inscrutable from one corner of my book-room? Its presence, first and foremost; even this replica has a force field—your eye is drawn to it, sitting in that room I feel as though I am not alone. Despite being unrealistic it is essentially catlike—not so much related to the comfortable complacent domestic cat we all know but to some more ancient, self-sufficient, prototype cat. I am reminded of the paper-thin feral cats of Cairo that I saw when last I went there, flitting the streets like ghost creatures. Perhaps they are just that, ghosts of all those cats turned into mummies in Pharaonic times—eviscerated, wrapped, stacked up in their thousands in animal cemeteries as tributes to the god.

I find myself responding to religions that recognize animals—that revere animals, indeed. Ancient Egypt above all, with each god having his or her own dedicated species. But it is universal in time and space, animal worship, animal respect. Christians and Muslims seem the only people to have abandoned it. We use animals—eat them, farm them, labor them—but we have lost touch with that elemental instinct to accord them status. We may abuse them less—in some parts of the world—but we can't any longer see them as totemic, as imbued with individual significance: ibis, crocodile, hawk, bull, bear, monkey, serpent. And cat. My cat reminds me of that loss.

It is an emblematic cat, then—essence of cat. And it is also, for me, a cat that resonates in time and space, within my own time-span and beyond; it speaks of that tall house in Harley Street, of a Mameluke house in Cairo, of a ship anchored off Gallipoli in 1915.

Elizabeth Barker's sampler

It is dated 1788. I doubt if Elizabeth Barker was a child; children usually give their age, on a sampler. No, a grown-up, I think, and while her sampler is not especially accomplished, it is pleasing, with text surrounded by stylized trees with birds and butterflies, and, below, two small stags and a pair of even smaller dogs, one brown, one black. It is the black dog that perhaps makes this my favorite sampler, along with the fact that it is the only one I have from the eighteenth century. The feisty little stitched black dog stands out, demanding attention from 1788.

At some point, way back, I thought I would start a sampler collection. I rapidly ran out of steam, partly because this proved a somewhat expensive undertaking, but also, I think, the commitment waned. So I have just eight samplers. I am still interested in, attracted by, samplers, but I feel a certain ambivalence. One of mine claims to be the work of: "Sarah Nottage. In her 7th year. 1836." I sincerely hope it wasn't. If six-year-old fingers really toiled over that canvas, made those tiny stitches, then that was child abuse. I hope—and suspect—that an adult hand helped out, at the very least.

Sarah's text is a standard one:

Food, raiment, dwelling, health and friends
Thou, Lord, has made our lot
With Thee our bliss begins and ends
As we are Thine, or not.

And so forth for two more verses . . . Piety is always the textual note.

Anna Maria Stacey, aged ten, in 1846, has:

Jesus permit thy gracious name to stand
As the first effort of an infant hand . . .

Which is straight out of the pattern books from which both texts and designs were taken. Pious sentiments, and formal designs of trees, flowers, animals, which may form a border round the edge, or motifs within. In a child's sampler, there is often an alphabet somewhere.

All of mine are fairly run-of-the-mill samplers. One is a map of England, another popular choice. All are worked in basic cross-stitch, and none have the elaborate originality of Victoria & Albert Museum quality samplers, as I realized when I looked into the matter once. In fact, the most interesting is perhaps the least immediately appealing—not well laid out, rather crudely worked. But the text is odd:

> Then ill [I'll] be not proud of my youth or my beauty since both of them wither and fade but [be?] in a good name by well doing my duty this will scent like a rose when I am dead.

Entirely secular; no religious sentiment. What is going on here? The next line is the key: "This was done at New Lanark School by Janet Martin aged 11 years. Finished her sampler 7 April 1813."

What is going on here is the first breath of

utopian socialism. Robert Owen—the industrialist and social reformer. New Lanark cotton mills in southern Scotland came under Owen's management in 1800. Thinker and philanthropist, he believed in the alleviation of poverty through socialism, and had conspicuously rejected formal religion: "all religions are based on the same ridiculous imagination, that make man a weak, imbecile animal; a furious bigot and fanatic; or a miserable hypocrite." So, no "Jesus permit thy gracious name to stand . . ." in his school, and the very existence of a school on that industrial site is a testimony to enlightenment.

I don't know where I acquired this, and I didn't realize its significance until some time later, deciphering that puzzling, awkwardly stitched text, and thinking: oh! New Lanark! Robert Owen! That sampler should be my favorite, for its historical and ideological freight, but I'm afraid Elizabeth Barker's little black dog has always elbowed it aside.

Samplers have had a further, personal relevance. My Somerset grandmother made one of her home and its setting, an exquisite, original design that shows the house, the garden pond with frogs and dragonflies, the white fantail pigeons, the dogs, the horses in the stables and, at the bottom, a row of small embroidered children—the wartime evacuees. She finished it in 1941, and it is my most treasured possession; an heirloom, indeed.

Furthermore, set against my routinely worked nineteenth-century samplers, this is in a different league. My grandmother's work is indeed of Victoria & Albert Museum quality.

Her design was creative, elaborate, ingenious. She used not just basic cross-stitch but a wide variety of stitches, thus giving depth and texture to her piece. And she worked with specially dyed wools in a subtle palette of blues, greens, buff, and a soft plum color.

Is this art or craft? And wherein lies the distinction, anyway? My grandmother had done fine needlework all her life: drawn-thread work, Assisi work with silks, Winchester wool work. The essence of this is craft, I suppose, but she had always created her own designs—not a pattern book in the house. And with the sampler it seems to me that craft segues into art, if what is implied is a grander concept, an enhanced vision. Her sampler is an embroidered painting, a fond and sometimes witty image of a place, executed with elegance and imagination. I am always a little awed by it, knowing I could never have aspired to such work myself.

The leaping fish sherd

It is about four inches across; it is slightly curved and is clearly the fragmented base of what has once been a wide, shallow dish, with the round

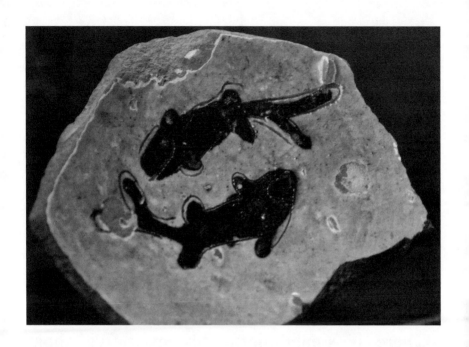

foot behind and the glazed surface above. The glaze is a rich honey color, and on it dance two small black fish. This sherd is twelfth century, possibly earlier, and came from Fustat, the first capital of Egypt, which is today a vast rubbish tip outside Cairo.

A friend gave me the sherd, twenty years or so ago, and it has sat on my mantelpiece ever since, relished for its survival, for its provenance, because it says that a potter a thousand years ago had seen fish leap, because it has traveled through time and space like this, ending up in twenty-first-century London, a signal from elsewhere.

The leaping fish cannot be later than twelfth century because Fustat was burned to the ground in 1168, an order given by its own Arab vizier so as to keep the wealth of the city from falling into the hands of the invading Crusaders. But they could be earlier, because Fustat had been the thriving capital since the seventh century, with a population of two hundred thousand by the time of its destruction. Artifacts from as far away as China have been excavated at Fustat, so it was trading, but it was itself a center for the manufacture of Islamic art and ceramics; whoever made the dish was in the business. Quite an expensive dish, I imagine, and perhaps there were more fish, or a further elaboration of the theme—other sea things.

There is something highly evocative about sherds—the detritus of the past. Crucial archaeological evidence, of course, and, if you are not an archaeologist, this vivid, tangible reminder of people who have been here before, making things and using them and discarding them. The past seems to echo with the sound of breaking crockery.

I am an archaeologist manquée, in a sense; that is the path I might have taken, had life run differently. It ran into fiction writing instead, but I do have a large cake tin full of sherds. Personal archaeology; garden archaeology, from the two old houses in which I have lived, one sixteenth-century, one seventeenth. We didn't acquire them for the sherd potential—I discovered that by degrees, as gardening enthusiasm grew, and my spade began to turn up items that invited close consideration. The sixteenth-century house had been a rectory, and its incumbents had clearly lived well: many oyster shells, and, most eloquent, chunks of the curved thick glass bases of eighteenth-century wine bottles. Both gardens threw up bowls and stem pieces of clay pipes. The clay pipe was tiresomely brittle, it seems; the past must echo also to expletives as yet another damn pipe fell to bits.

The seventeenth-century garden yielded most—perhaps because it was there that the most intense vegetable growing took place, in an area that had been the farmyard. Much deep digging on my part, the fruits of which have filled the cake tin. Blue and white willow-pattern china in quantities, which probably dates from late eighteenth century to early twentieth. Other china—particularly pretty green and white fluted sherds with a floral design, remains of some treasured best tea or dinner service, I decided. And, reaching further back in time, a couple of sherds of seventeenth-century salt glaze—the deep yellow glaze with scribbled lines and loops in dark brown. And a fragment of broken handle in the other kind of salt glaze—mottled brown. Much plain earthenware, evidently from large crocks and smaller ones. And there was some glazed earthenware mottled with green that looked like the medieval pots in the Ashmolean and, if so, might have dated from even before the construction of the farmhouse in 1620. An entire sequence of domestic crockery, silent testimony lying there in that richly fertile soil— "scarce below the roots of some vegetables," as Sir Thomas Browne put it. My vegetables, now.

There were other tantalizing finds. A tiny green glass bottle, just over an inch high. Nineteenth century, by the look of it. But what could it have held? And a little, delicate, cream-colored horn spoon; another valued item, surely, lost rather than discarded.

This was not archaeology, of course. It was fortuitous discovery. And these homely Oxfordshire finds seem a far cry from the exotic implications of the leaping fish sherd. But, for me, all fed into an insatiable fascination with what has been, what is gone but survives in these glimpses afforded by something you can hold in your hand, these suggestions of other people who also held this, used it, made it.

It is not enough to live here and now. Not enough for me, anyway. I need those imaginative leaps out of my own time frame and into other places— places where things were done differently. Reading has provided me with that, for the most part, but it is objects, things like these scraps of pottery, that have most keenly conjured up all those elsewheres—inaccessible but eerily available to the imagination. The past is irretrievable, but it lurks. It sends out tantalizing messages, coded signals in the form of a clay pipe stem, a smashed wine bottle. Two leaping fish from twelfth-century Cairo. I can't begin to understand what that time was like, or how the men who made them lived, but I can know that it all happened—that old Cairo existed, and a particular potter. To have the leaping fish sherd on my mantelpiece—and all those other sherds in the cake tin—expands my concept of time. There is a further dimension to memory; it is not just a private asset, but something vast, collective, resonant. And all because fragments of detritus survive, and I can consider them.

Penelope Lively is the author of many prize-winning novels and short-story collections for both adults and children. She has twice been short-listed for the Booker Prize: once in 1977 for her first novel, *The Road to Lichfield*, and again in 1984 for *According to Mark*. She later won the 1987 Booker Prize for her highly acclaimed novel *Moon Tiger*. Her other books include *Going Back*; *Judgement Day*; *Next to Nature, Art*; *Perfect Happiness*; *Passing On*; *City of the Mind*; *Cleopatra's Sister*; *Heat Wave*; *Beyond the Blue Mountains*, a collection of short stories; *Oleander, Jacaranda*, a memoir of her childhood days in Egypt; *Spiderweb*; her autobiographical work *A House Unlocked*; *The Photograph*; *Making It Up*; *Consequences*; *Family Album*, which was short-listed for the 2009 Costa Novel Award; and *How It All Began*. She is a popular writer for children and has won both the Carnegie Medal and the Whitbread Award. She was appointed CBE in the 2001 New Year's Honours List, and was made a dame in 2012. She lives in London.

Center Point Large Print
600 Brooks Road / PO Box 1
Thorndike ME 04986-0001 USA

(207) 568-3717

US & Canada:
1 800 929-9108
www.centerpointlargeprint.com